Healing Guides

Tarot

THE MODERN BOOK
OF DIVINATION

 **SparkPool**

INTRODUCTION

Do you have questions about your life that you would love to have answered? Do you wish that you could learn more about yourself and what makes you happy? Then tarot could be the tool you have been looking for. Using tarot cards can be incredibly insightful: it's a little like holding up a mirror to your innermost self. It allows you to reach into your subconscious mind, or inner wisdom, to find answers to questions about your life. The cards can help you to investigate yourself, learn more about who you are and tap into your intuition. And by doing so, you can begin to turn your dreams and goals into reality.

If you are someone who has burning questions about your destiny, perhaps relating to your relationships, your career, your finances and more, you may have come into possession of this book to investigate yourself and who you really are. The beauty of tarot is that through self-exploration with the cards, it's possible to discover things that you may not have been fully aware of. And through that discovery, you can begin to build and shape a life that works for you.

Tarot may hold negative connotations to some, such as the association with the Devil, or the idea that tarot reading relates to the summoning of evil spirits. But these are simply common misconceptions. While tarot cards have often been linked to the occult and 'dark arts', the power they possess is simply unlocked through the intuition and open-mindedness of the reader or the querent.

The story of tarot

The use of tarot came about in the fourteenth century, when European artists began painting playing cards for recreational purposes. Over time, the use of cards for divination became more and more popular as people began to attribute meaning and symbolism to each unique design. Fast forward to the present day, and tarot is an established practice which continues to grow in popularity. In an increasingly uncertain world, traditional religions sometimes no longer hold all the answers for many members of society. Let's face it: the challenges of modern life can often lead us to question the meaning of it! So, some are turning to alternative belief systems to help them manage the stormy waters of their bustling lives.

What is tarot?

To understand tarot, it helps to first explore the cards. A tarot is a deck of 78 cards, each of which display imagery, symbolism and a story. There are 22 Major Arcana cards, which represent lessons that are learnt through life. 56 Minor Arcana cards represent the everyday difficulties that people may experience. Within those 56 cards are 16 tarot court cards, which represent 16 personality characteristics. Also within the Minor Arcana cards are 4 suits, with 10 cards within each. They represent different situations that are often encountered by people.

Okay, so that's a physical explanation of the cards, but what is a little trickier to unravel is how the cards actually work. Well, when the cards are selected and laid out front of you, you can take the opportunity to observe and interpret them. And that is where the tarot magic happens: the imagery stimulates the creative part of your brain so that you are more receptive to thoughts and ideas about yourself. The images help you to connect with your inner wisdom and self-knowledge. And by connecting with them, you can make positive changes in your life that help you achieve goals and desired outcomes. Now, that's an amazing power to have!

HOW TO USE THIS BOOK

Are you ready to tap into tarot and discover just how powerful the cards can be? Then let's get started. In this book you'll learn how to use tarot cards and how to read them. And ultimately, you'll learn how to harness your newfound skills to carry out readings for others. But, as with the start of any new journey, beginning with some important basics is key.

Choosing your deck

Finding a deck of tarot cards that is right for you is essential. There are hundreds of different tarot decks available, and to a newcomer, choosing one could feel overwhelming. But choosing the perfect deck might be easier than you think. Here are some tips for finding your perfect cards:

1. Explore! Check out the tarot decks of friends or influential tarot experts and find out what you like or dislike.

2. Visit shops and look at and touch the decks there. See what style or design appeals to you. If you don't like a deck, pass it by. If one calls to you, it could very well be the one you need

3. Take time choosing. Don't feel rushed into buying your first deck. It is important that you feel comfortable with the cards and like them.

Keeping your deck safe

Once you have chosen your cards, you need to protect them from physical damage and any negative energy. It is pretty easy to do this. Great techniques are to wrap the cards in a silk scarf or put them in a small box, then put them somewhere safe, where no one else will find or touch them. You can also buy drawstring pouches that you can drop your cards into and then seal off with a pull-tie. Or you could make a simple cotton or silk bag or a velvet pouch and decorate it to make it totally your own with embroidery, charms and fabric paint, for example. Your tarot cards won't wear out as quickly if you store the pack correctly and if you use a spread cloth for each reading you perform. Protecting your cards from physical harm and negative energy is essential because this could affect your readings.

Get to know your cards

It's important to build a relationship with your cards before you start to use them. You can do this simply by spending time with them. It may sound unusual, but sleeping with your cards under your pillow is a great place to start. People who use tarot believe that while you are asleep, your subconscious gives off energy that the cards will easily absorb. That will connect you to them in a powerful and profound way.

Moving on

In the rest of this book, you'll learn how to use your deck and interpret the cards. Working with tarot is an exciting voyage, and one that can't be rushed. Just like any relationship, your connection with your cards will grow over time and you'll learn more about them. So take time to explore each chapter carefully and learn what this amazing practice has to offer. Travel slowly on your tarot journey, and you'll enjoy the ride!

MYTHS ABOUT TAROT AND CARING FOR YOUR DECK

Before you start using your tarot cards, it's important to clear the air and get rid of a few of the myths and misconceptions about tarot cards that are out there.

Myth busters

Here are three of the most common myths and misconceptions, debunked:

1. No, you don't have to be psychic to read tarot cards. There are no supernatural powers involved that help you see the future or contact the spirit world. Anyone can learn to read tarot. All people need to do is to listen to their intuition.

2. Tarot readers are not fortune tellers and the cards are not magic. Tarot cards can show you the direction you're heading based on where you are now and that gives you the choice whether to follow that path or reshape your future. The magic of tarot cards lies in the way the user of the cards handles them.

3. No, the Death card *does not* mean someone is going to die. This myth is one of the most common. Of course death is inevitable and we will all die at some point, but the Death card absolutely does not signify imminent doom. It usually indicates a change is coming. Change can be difficult, but changes are inevitable and they can also bring good things and a better life.

The power of tarot

A deck of tarot cards is really like a tool to help people open up and talk about things. Tarot readings are more like an in-depth conversation between two people, which the cards and their implied meanings help to inspire. Perhaps, because there's a little mystical energy or mystery to the cards, people open up in a way that they might not otherwise do in a normal conversation. A lot of people feel like the tarot cards bring a special, positive energy that breaks down barriers and helps them to be more open about themselves, their worries, their dreams and their desires.

Energy in a reading

Tarot cards work with your energy and intuition. When you shuffle a deck, you transfer energy into the cards so that when you turn or draw cards in a reading, those cards are most relevant for you. Every tarot card has images and symbols that help you connect to your intuitive mind when you look at them. For example, a cup overflowing might put you in mind of a time you felt overwhelmed. Or maybe the story behind those images echoes something of what you're currently experiencing or feeling. Tarot works by understanding the present to predict the future. You react to the cards and if the cards show an outcome that is not what you want, you can take action to change your future.

Caring for your deck

Protecting your cards from physical harm and negative energy is important, because it could affect the energy in your readings. Try to avoid letting others touch the cards too. If your deck is exposed to unwanted energy, don't worry – you can cleanse it. Many tarot users swear by using crystals to absorb energies around their cards. You can place a quartz crystal near your cards to absorb any negative energies you feel are affecting your readings. Amethyst, rose quartz, selenite, citrine and tiger's eye are all wonderful crystals for cleansing the cards.

Some people regularly cleanse their tarot cards and related tools, such as tarot bags and reading area or spread cloths, by smudging. Smudging is the practice of cleansing something with the smoke of a herb, often sage. It's simple to do. Open the doors and windows and then light a bunch of sage. This is your smudge stick. Smudge your items by wafting the smoke around them while thinking about how this is cleansing them. Extinguish the smudge stick by dropping it in a metal bowl. Job done.

TAROT CARDS AND THEIR SYMBOLISM

There are no strict rules in tarot because it is an intuitive practice, but learning more about the tarot's symbolism and associations can help you understand your tarot readings in a new way.

Tarot's links to the zodiac

Each sign of the zodiac is linked to a card in the Major Arcana. The tarot card that is associated with your zodiac sign will have similar traits or images to those of your zodiac sign.

- **Aries:** The Emperor
- **Taurus:** The Hierophant
- **Gemini:** The Lovers
- **Cancer:** The Chariot
- **Leo:** Strength
- **Virgo:** The Hermit

- **Libra:** Justice
- **Scorpio:** Death
- **Sagittarius:** Temperance
- **Capricorn:** The Devil
- **Aquarius:** The Star
- **Pisces:** The Moon

You can find out more about these particular Major Arcana cards in the next section of the book. Knowing which zodiac sign and tarot card are connected can add an extra dimension to a tarot reading. For example, your tarot card might represent you or if you see your partner's, friend's, or relative's tarot card in a reading, that might add a new level of understanding to an interpretation.

Number meanings in the Minor Arcana

The Minor Arcana includes four suits, each of which includes ten number cards with particular meanings attributed to each number. How do the number meanings influence the Minor Arcana suits? Let's dive in and find out.

- **Ace (one):** opportunity, initiation, a new start, leading, ambition, originality
- **Two:** duality, togetherness, settled energy, union, love, balance
- **Three:** expression, expansion of an idea, growth, first stages of completion
- **Four:** form, completeness, foundations, progress, power, stability
- **Five:** instability, exaggeration, over-exertion, strife, changes, freedom, loss, difficulties, struggle to access the 'good'
- **Six:** movement, balance, solutions, harmony, healing, empathy, a mid-point, change, communication
- **Seven:** regaining or losing control, mastery, choices, responsibility, myth, secrets, personal attainment, practical advice
- **Eight:** manifestation, practicality, skill, achievement, absolute decisions, business, the ego
- **Nine:** the feeling of being 'almost there', encouragement or a warning, strength, compassion, optimism, suffering
- **Ten:** fulfilment, ultimate completion, final manifestation, result of true will, recognition, continuation, realisation, endings

The Elements and the Minor Arcana cards

To read tarot you need to understand the four elements that are associated with the tarot suits of the Minor Arcana. These are Water, Fire, Earth and Air. These elements give a specific type of energy to each suit.

Water is symbolic of fluidity, feelings and emotions, intuition, relationships, healing and cleansing and is linked to the suit of Cups. Cups cards are linked to creativity, romanticism, fantasy and imagination and suggest you're thinking with your heart rather than your head.

Fire represents passion, energy, enthusiasm, willpower, drive and sexuality. It is linked to the suit of Wands. Wand cards are about our personalities, egos, enthusiasms, ideas about ourselves and personal energy.

Earth is grounded, stable, supportive and fertile and is linked to the suit of Pentacles. Pentacles represent the material aspects of life such as work, business, trade, property, money and material possessions and how we interact with these and how they affect our self-esteem and self-image.

The Air element relates to knowledge, action, power and change and links to the suit of Swords. Swords are linked with action, change, force, power, oppression, ambition, courage and conflict.

Colours on the cards

There are many different kinds of tarot packs and some will use different colour meanings. Our reactions to colours can be quite an individual thing, but this list gives you a starting point to learn the significance of different colours on the cards.

- **White:** purity, beginnings and newness
- **Black:** negativity, hidden things and ignorance
- **Red:** energy, patience, activity, passion and vitality
- **Yellow:** spirituality and intellect
- **Green:** humanity, growth and early changes
- **Blue:** intuition, emotion, healing and peace
- **Brown:** being down to earth and practical
- **Orange:** courage and vitality
- **Pale Orange:** jealousy
- **Grey:** wisdom

GETTING DOWN TO BUSINESS

Tarot is a great way to gain insight into questions you may have about your life, but before embarking on a reading there are a few more things you need to know, from creating an atmosphere to shuffling.

Keep calm and carry on

A calm, soothing atmosphere allows for an open, receptive mind, and that's just what you want for a good tarot reading. Find a space that is relaxed and welcoming for reading. Make sure it is warm and cosy and ideally has some beautiful pictures or fabrics around and plenty of light. You might like to light some incense to scent the air and some people even like to put on some very gentle mood music, very quietly. Do some controlled breathing exercises to centre and calm yourself before you start.

Do the shuffle

The way you actually shuffle the cards doesn't really matter, it's what you do while shuffling them that counts. Before you start shuffling, hold the cards in your hands and think about the question you'd like guidance on. This is the moment to ask the cards, out loud or in your mind, if now is the right time to leave that job, if your crush is the one, or anything else that is troubling you. Then, while continuing to focus on that question, shuffle and mix the cards in whatever way feels right to you. It's a means of transferring your energy over to the cards and getting into a mindset in which you step out of everyday life and reach a more intuitive frame of mind.

Two-card spread

For a fast reading that takes just a minute or two to do, but can give lots of insight and clarity, try this simple two-card cross. Shuffle your cards, closing your eyes and keeping your question in mind. Take a few slow, deep breaths as you do so. When you're ready, lay the first card. Lay a second card sideways across it; the first card represents the core of your question, the situation itself, and the second card represents something that is 'crossing' you, a challenge you're facing or a weight you're carrying, or something else that is affecting your situation and needs attention.

Three-card spread

A simple option for a three-card spread is to lay the three cards in a row. The first represents the past, the second the present and the third the future or a final outcome. The past card can include past events, or the feelings of the querent and other people that have had an impact on the current situation. The centre card symbolises the things that are happening right now and it can relate to how the querent or others experience or view the situation, and includes things like external influences and hidden obstacles. The third card could represent a long-term goal or an immediate resolution, depending on the question and the situation that the querent is facing.

Five-card spread

A five-card horseshoe tarot spread is a really good way to answer a specific question and find guidance for your or the querent's life about a certain topic. As its name suggests, the five-card horseshoe spread is laid out in a horseshoe shape with the first three cards facing upwards, and the last two facing downwards on the opposite side. The first card refers to past influences. These are things that affect the situation you are in right now. The second card reflects your present situation and what you hope to get out of it. The third card reflects any unexpected issues that may pop up that you need to know about. The fourth card gives you advice and guidance on the best course of action you can take right now. The fifth card refers to the outcome of the situation.

Twelve-card spread

It can be fun to do a twelve-month reading to get some insight into what the year ahead holds. Lay down twelve cards in a circle, clockwise, starting with the card representing January at the top. Then lay them face down at first and then flip them over, starting from the top. Then sit with each card and note what it brings up from the depths of your subconscious. With this many cards, it can be helpful to have a notepad or journal nearby to jot down your thoughts. This will also help you see patterns emerge, in case any ideas don't immediately make sense to you.

Thirteen-card spread

This spread is complicated and may be easier if you know something about astrology and horoscopes. It's also best done infrequently, perhaps four times a year at most.

Once you shuffle and cut the deck, the first card is placed at the far left, at the nine o'clock position. The remaining cards are laid anti-clockwise in a circle, one at each hour of the clock. Put the thirteenth card in the centre. Each of the thirteen positions has a specific meaning that leads you through the reading:

1. **Aries** represents how the individual normally works through difficulties

2. **Taurus** refers to the current financial situation, or it may relate to feelings about practical matters, such as money, but not relate directly to finances

3. **Gemini** can indicate how an individual communicates and what could be done differently

4. **Cancer** relates to either a physical or emotional home and might describe the need for emotional security, or the search for a physical home

5. **Leo** controls romance, art and pleasure, and should be read in conjunction with Libra and Capricorn

6. **Virgo** indicates health, whether it's physical, spiritual, emotional or mental

7. **Libra** refers to romantic or business relationships, or simple friendships, and should be read in conjunction with the Leo card

8. **Scorpio** deals with either an emotional issue or a firm objective linked to sex, money or death

9. **Sagittarius** indicates education, hope and changes in attitudes or beliefs

10. **Capricorn** reveals ambition, drive and talent, and can also refer to work

11. **Aquarius** refers to the friends already present in an individual's life, or what is hoped for in the future

12. **Pisces** is the card of vulnerability and reveals hidden hopes and secret fears, while also pointing to blocks or obstacles to success

13. Final Outcome indicates the ultimate outcome of the entire situation in a six-month time frame

MAJOR ARCANA

The Major Arcana features 22 cards numbered 0 to 21, and they represent big life lessons and energies. The Major Arcana, as its grandiose name suggests, is a big deal. It's about the big issues in life. The cards in the Major Arcana represent experiences such as defying or resisting authority, falling in love, or getting unexpected bad or life-changing news. These 22 tarot cards include some of the most recognisable in decks across the world: The Lovers, The Devil and The High Priestess, to name a few.

The story in the cards

Each one of the Major Arcana cards can stand alone and has its own important meanings and power, but the 22 cards collectively tell a single story. The Fool, the first card in the Major Arcana, or card 0, is the main character of this story. The following 21 cards take us on The Fool's journey as he makes his way through the world. His experiences as he meets different figures and challenges along the way help him to learn, change and grow. Cards such as Love, Strength, The Hanged Man and Justice represent important archetypes, or typical examples of the accomplishments, setbacks and lessons we all learn as we go through life and encounter all the ordeals and challenges the world throws at us. The idea is that we, like The Fool, grow as we progress along our journey until we become whole, complete beings by the end of it.

The Fool

First stop in the tarot hall of fame is The Fool, but this card isn't as half-baked as its name suggests. Being foolish can be a good thing: think spontaneous, open to possibilities, up for a laugh, full of excitement. The Fool is a mostly positive card that suggests new beginnings and is a sign of unlimited potential. Thinking of a new adventure or a big trip? Maybe drawing The Fool is the sign it's your time to shine!

Upright

Drawing The Fool upright means, 'Go for it!' A fool's naivety or inexperience can be a virtue. Fools don't get weighed down by memories of past failures. Grasp that optimism with both hands and live for the moment. This card is all about taking a chance – who knows where saying 'yes' to a new challenge could lead you? Don't overthink it or get bogged down with the risks and consequences. New experiences help us to grow and evolve, even if things don't go perfectly. Sometimes the unexpected things that happen to us make us happiest and open doors to new opportunities that change our lives. Of course, if you go for it, something may go wrong. There are no guarantees in life. But at least if you try, you get to enjoy the ride and see where it leads you.

Reversed

The reversed Fool card is all about letting go of the baggage that weighs you down and holds you back. If you've had some bad luck or failures, the chances are you're burdened by your own negativity. Some people never try a new direction because they're so sure it'll end in disaster, so why bother? The problem is, talking yourself out of taking chances means you're bound to miss out on opportunities.

A note of caution... drawing The Fool reversed can also mean take a breath. You wouldn't step off a diving board before checking there's water in the pool, would you? So, consider the consequences of your actions. Is it a risk worth taking? Do your research instead of acting on the spur of the moment.

The Magician

Abracadabra! Drawing The Magician tarot card is a sign that it's time for you to tap into your own magical powers! The Magician is a Major Arcana card that can grant your wishes if you take action and use some of your own talents, determination and willpower. The Magician stands with one hand pointing to the sky and the other pointing to the ground, showing how he can connect the spiritual and the real worlds. The Magician's table holds all the suits of the tarot and all of its power: a cup, pentacle, a sword and a wand.

Upright

Drawing The Magician card upright means you have all the tools right under your nose to manifest your goals, whether that's in love, work, new intentions or any other realm of your life. Magic is at your fingertips – you just have to reach out and touch it! The Magician says you have the determination and willpower to make your wishes and dreams come true. It is the time for you to take action. Work out what you want and why, and find out what you've got to do to attain your goals. Make a plan and stay focused. If you are learning a new skill, stay with it. Persevere and practise. You've got the power – use it!

Reversed

The reversed Magician tells you you're letting something hold you back from achieving your desires. Have you left the door open to self-doubt or apathy? Is imposter syndrome tying you down? Boss up! Ditch the excuses and get out of your own way. It's better to try and fail than not try at all. Dig deep and find that self-belief: trust that you have the tools and talents, and start to use them.

The Magician is all about power, so if the card is reversed, it could also mean you're using your power in the wrong way. Are you trying to achieve your goals using negative means, like manipulation or sneakiness? Getting ahead that way won't bring you the satisfaction or results you desire. Follow a path that is honest and stay true to yourself.

The High Priestess

The High Priestess is the epitome of girl power. She is sometimes called 'The Wise Woman' card and she looks like someone who's got all the answers. The High Priestess is powerful yet mysterious, serene and wise, sensual and spiritual. She is seated because this is a card of non-action. She's all about assessing situations, about taking time to withdraw from a situation and reflect upon it before going any further. This card is about trusting your instincts to guide you. Sit back and give yourself the space and time to listen to your own inner voice. Solve your own mysteries!

Upright

Drawing an upright High Priestess card usually means it's time to look inward rather than outward, to get the guidance that you need. Listen to your intuition. Slow down and think about what you've learnt before making a decision or taking action. If you're facing a big decision or a difficult choice, the High Priestess wants you to dive headfirst into your subconscious mind so that answers can flow freely from within. Use your energy and time to reflect on what you've learnt and to prepare yourself for all possible outcomes. Once the outcome is clear, you'll be ready to act upon it.

Reversed

The High Priestess reversed card may be a sign that you're repressing your own feelings and that you're finding it hard to trust your gut. Do you overthink things and forget to listen to your own intuition? Or are you too easily swayed by other people's opinions instead of listening to your own inner voice? The reversed High Priestess card could be a timely reminder to stand firm in your own beliefs. You know what's best for you! You don't need other people telling you what to do. Instead, find a quiet spot and look for the answers within. Relax! You've got this. Trust your gut and let it lead you to the right answers.

The Empress

If you're starting a new job or business, diving into an exciting new project, or even planning a family, then The Empress is one of the cards you want to see at a tarot reading. The Empress is nurturing, creative and appreciative. She is a symbol of growth and fertility, but not only in the sense of motherhood. She's all about helping you develop and cheering you on in everyday life and in any venture you're hoping to find success in. She's like your biggest supporter and fan who wants the best for you, sees the very best you have to offer and encourages you to reach your full potential.

Upright

Drawing an upright Empress card is a reminder to be mindful and make the most of each and every experience. Connect with your senses and make every day special – you deserve it! So dress your best, even if you're just going to the corner shop to get some milk. Buy yourself some fresh flowers and make time for that bubble bath, even if there are chores waiting to be done. The Empress also encourages you to get creative, so this may be the perfect time to take up a new hobby like painting, music, drama or other art forms that let you express yourself creatively.

Reversed

A reversed Empress card suggests your energy is running low and you've been too busy tending to the needs of other people to look after your own. It's good to care about other people and help them too, but you can't do this at the expense of your own emotional needs. The Empress reversed card encourages you to make self-love and self-care your priority. Taking care of yourself also feeds in to how you care for others.

The Empress reversed card can also be about encouraging you to find your own creativity or success. Don't be held back by other people's expectations or your feelings of inadequacy. Just sit back, relax, and let your creativity flow. You'll only be able to thrive and develop if you give yourself the space to do so.

The Emperor

Boss it up! The Emperor tarot card is all about power. The Emperor represents a figure in your life who is wise, a leader that perhaps brings stability and balance. It could be a parent, manager at work or a partner. This figure could be male or female, or it could even represent you if you are looking to take on more responsibilities. The key words when looking at an Emperor tarot card are strength, leadership, rules, order and structure. The key to a tarot reading with this card is to work out who it refers to and the way that person uses their power.

Upright

An upright Emperor card can offer clarity on a number of different situations. For example, if you're in a relationship, perhaps the card represents a partner who has a little too much power in your dynamic? Do you feel comfortable speaking up for yourself? Does your partner always have the last word in an argument? Maybe it's time to find your voice or set better boundaries for yourself.

At work, The Emperor card could represent the boss who likes structure, rules and order, or it could represent yourself. Is your leadership style working for you? Is it weak, and do other people walk over you? If so, take control. Or are you throwing your weight around a little too much? Don't be a tyrant, let the rules and structures you make do the talking.

Reversed

Drawing The Emperor reversed can be a reminder to find your strength if you're in a situation when you feel like giving up. You're the boss! Say yes to that promotion or get some career advice or mentoring to help you move on up. An Emperor reversed can mean you or your partner are not ready to level up your relationship status. Maybe you or they aren't quite ready to commit yet, or maybe you're wrong for each other. That's for you to work out.

The Hierophant

The Hierophant is like the Yoda of the tarot card realm. The Hierophant shares their wisdom and knowledge with others and guides them to make the right choices. It represents tradition, spiritual guidance and conformity. But that doesn't mean toeing the line and following rules blindly. It's about keeping traditions and rules that are tried and tested and true, but also questioning authority if needs be and marching to the beat of your own drum instead. If, on reflection, those rules or traditions suck, you can make some new ones!

Upright

The idea of age-old traditions, longstanding rules and guidelines can all conjure up feelings of oppressiveness or being stuck in the past. But they have an important role to play. We humans are social animals and sharing an understanding about fair and just ways of doing things can help us live alongside each other safely and happily. To live and function in any community, we must have rules and guidelines we mostly all agree on so we can understand how to function as part of a group. It doesn't matter if you're part of a workforce, coven, large family or band, accepting what our roles are and what is expected of us can help to make us feel part of something bigger than ourselves and that's a good thing.

Reversed

A reversed Hierophant card is all about questioning authority. It's about standing up for what you want and believe in, even if it means stepping outside the rules or going against what other people think and expect you to do. So what if that regular job pays a regular wage? If you want to take a chance and have a go at being a part-time potter instead, then go for it. And just because everyone else thinks you should stay with that nice guy, why not take a chance on new love? Drawing a Hierophant reversed card is the universe's way of telling you to wake up and trust your instincts. Follow your own path, even if it's not the conventional one.

The Lovers

Love, love, love... Just as there are more songs written about love than any other subject, there are more takers for a tarot card reading about love than any other topic. The Lovers card is all about relationships, but it's not just about finding the one. The Lovers card is also about knowing yourself and what you want and need from all kinds of relationships, whether they are lovers, friends or even work colleagues. It's about knowing yourself and your true worth so that you can make the choices that are right for you.

Upright

There are two lovers on The Lovers card and the key to a good relationship is two-way communication. You can't just let the other person dictate your decisions, choices and values for you. For a balanced and happy relationship, you need to be honest about how you feel and what you need. As well as being able to express yourself, and to be able to hear their voice, you need to know that the other person hears and understands you too. We can only find true unity and togetherness when we can really say how we feel. The best way to achieve intimacy and commitment is through the trust and mutual respect that comes from honest communication.

Reversed

The reversed Lovers card tells you all is not right in paradise. Something is off balance or out of place. Maybe you've been neglecting your friends and personal life while you chase that promotion. Or perhaps you've been letting someone else get their way because you're too afraid you'll upset them if you express your needs? You know what the problem is. Now it's time to set things right. If you've messed up, own it, apologise and make a change. If you know you need to be true to yourself, speak up. Make things right and bring romance and harmony back into your life.

———◆———

The Chariot

Buckle up – it's going to be a bumpy ride! A chariot is a two-wheeled vehicle that was used in ancient times for racing and fighting. Chariots carry you to where you want to go. The Chariot tarot card turns up when someone is ready to make a big decision or take a big step, but hasn't done so yet for some reason. Chariots are associated with forward movement and The Chariot card means that it's time to look ahead, make that move, and focus on the future. Your destiny is in your own hands. You are in charge of your fate and you can determine what you get out of life.

Upright

An upright Chariot card is a great one to draw when you're facing a big decision. If you're having a tarot reading to ask questions about a relationship, a career or a house move, for example, drawing The Chariot card is the equivalent of hearing the race whistle that tells you to take your mark, get set and go! It should help you to feel empowered to take that next big step forward. It won't necessarily be easy, but you can go ahead with more confidence, reassured that the changes you make will be for the better.

Reversed

A reversed Chariot tarot card can mean, 'Hold your horses'. Put on the brakes and take some time to think about whether you're making the correct choice or decision. Check your facts and feelings. Are you really ready for this change? Do you need to do some more research, preparation or soul-searching before charging ahead? Are you truly geared up and fully trained for this particular battle? The Chariot card reversed may mean you need to take more time and do a little more work before committing to that relationship, changing jobs or handing in that project.

The Tower

Just not feeling it at the moment? The Tower tarot card presents an image of power and strength being struck down. The Tower is starting to crumble and fall. This card is often drawn when things are falling apart in someone's life or when they know the foundations of a relationship or situation in their life are unstable. The Tower represents an unsettled period of change. Expect the unexpected! The good news is that while it's true something is going to be changed, destroyed or lost, something better is going to take its place.

Upright

Drawing an upright Tower card is the universe's way of telling you that something is disintegrating or falling apart in your life. Some part of your life is built on unstable ground. It could be a relationship that's struggling, a career you chose that turned out not to be what you hoped it would be, or some belief in your life that isn't holding true. Did you let a chance for improvement slip through your fingers? This card is telling you it's time to shake things up!

The upright Tower card is the impetus you need to make that change and seize a transformation. Okay, you will have to deal with some upheaval and chaos, but whatever form the crumbling Tower represents in your life, it wasn't going to stay standing for long, so become your own tower of strength and reach within for inspiration to embrace the new when the old has fallen.

Reversed

A Tower reversed card can mean the chaos you feel is coming from within. Are you so anxious about inevitable change that you are refusing to see that change is coming or has already begun? Be honest with yourself. What is it in your life that has unstable foundations? Is there something you think is solid and strong, but which really isn't? Maybe you are making yourself believe that job, relationship or direction is right for you, when really you know it's doomed to failure?

The Star

Stars are beacons of light in the darkness. And The Star tarot card is a reminder that there is light in your life even on the darkest days. People often draw The Star card at a point when things are going wrong in their life. It's a cosmic reminder to keep the faith and trust that things will be okay again. Have hope. You have the power to heal yourself. The Star is a blessing from the universe and provides inspiration that things will get better as you move forwards.

Upright

Drawing The Star card upright is a sign that your star is rising. Yes, times may have been tough recently, but the future looks bright. Thank your lucky stars for the healing that's already underway. Reach for the stars and find the inspiration you need. You can do anything. You just need to believe in yourself and believe that there are good things waiting around the corner. Think about what went wrong and how it affected you, but don't beat yourself up for any mistakes. Find peace and acceptance for who you are. If help comes your way, accept it and try to help others as you move forwards into a new day with hope and love.

Reversed

A reversed Star card suggests you are finding it difficult to spot those twinkling lights of hope in the darkness of your despair. Things can feel pretty miserable and hopeless sometimes. Don't give up. The Star card is a reminder that good, new things are out there for you. Hardships teach us a lot about ourselves, so find your strength and be proud of how you keep moving forwards. Embrace the opportunity to build something new. When woes and worries are weighing us down, The Star reversed card tells us to take some time to recharge our batteries and practise some self-care. You'll know when you're ready to shoot for the stars again.

The Moon

Have you ever noticed you have trouble sleeping, concentrating or keeping calm during a full moon? It's common to feel this way because the energy of the full moon stirs up your emotions. The full moon can feel like a bit of a disruptive time. The Moon tarot card shines a light on our deepest anxieties and concerns. It often appears at a time when we feel confused or overwhelmed by life, to help us work through our feelings and find a way through the mayhem.

Upright

The upright Moon card is here to tell you it's okay to feel scared, anxious, overwhelmed and confused sometimes. If something is stressing you out, work out how to fix the problem. If you have a difficult decision to make, find out more about your options. This will empower you and clear the fog in your mind. Hit the pause button and take what time you need to work things out.

Sometimes you need to dig deeper to find solutions. Maybe you need to slow down and look deep into yourself to learn what the real problem is. What are your feelings and instincts telling you? Do solutions present themselves to you in your dreams?

Reversed

The Moon reversed card suggests you are at the point of releasing your fear, repressed emotions or confusion. The negative energy around you is clearing. If your anxiety has been caused by someone's lies, the truth will be revealed. The only thing stopping you shooting for the Moon is an illusion. An illusion is something that deceives by producing a false or misleading impression of reality. Work out what is real and what your illusions are. Which of your ideas about yourself or your situation are not actually true? Tackle and dismantle your illusions so that you can move forwards again.

The Sun

Who doesn't feel better when they wake up to morning sunshine? The Sun radiates joy, happiness and optimism. It literally lights up our world. The Sun tarot card is a reminder to seek the light even on our darkest days. It's telling us that no matter how tough things are, there is light at the end of the tunnel, so keep positive and try to be grateful for the good things in our lives. Bad luck can turn to good luck with the dawn. If things are feeling too much or you're feeling down, look up to the sky and soak up some of the Sun's positive energy.

Upright

Drawing an upright Sun card means it's your time to shine. Make like the Sun and radiate the confidence, optimism and joy you hold within. Don't stay in the shadows or let other people dampen your fire. You're having a moment so enjoy it. Think about the things you've achieved or that make you proud. What good luck has come your way? Bask in the warm glow of success. Feel good about yourself and notice the way other people are enchanted or fascinated by you when you shine brightly like this.

Reversed

Do you feel as if there's a dark cloud following you around? Are you feeling overwhelmed, lost or suffering setbacks? The reversed Sun card is here to tell you everything will work out. It's a fact of life that we will all have bad days and hit bumps in the road, but just as the Sun rises every morning to chase away the darkness, good things lie ahead for you too. The reversed Sun card encourages you to keep going and trust things will get better. Try to be thankful for what you have already achieved and the joys you already have in your life, however small they feel right now, while looking forwards to the day that will follow this night.

— ☼ —

Strength

The word 'strength' conjures up images of muscles and weights, but The Strength tarot card is all about inner strength. It's about having the strength of your convictions and beliefs to do the right thing. It's about standing firm and keeping going when things get difficult. The Strength card is about strength of character. This card reminds us to play to our strengths, to know your own strength and to keep working on that inner power.

Upright

A Strength upright card is telling you that you've got the power! You are a pillar of strength, whether you're aware of it or not. It's time for you to be confident and courageous and make the changes and take the chances you know are right for you. Feel reassured that you can make the right choices for yourself. That could mean changing jobs if the one you're in isn't right for you. Or it could mean trusting that you will find love and you are deserving of it, even if it hasn't come along yet. You deserve the best, so make it happen or hold out for it.

Reversed

Drawing The Strength card in reverse suggests your own fears and anxieties may be holding you back from the life you want. Perhaps you're finding it hard to find the courage and inner strength you need to overcome those fears? A reversed Strength card is offering you the chance to do something about this. What can you do to unblock your power? Take your time. It's okay to take baby steps at first. The important thing is that you are looking at where those fears come from and how they are impacting your life. That way you will be able to control those fears and harness your strength to combat them and the situations or problems you face ahead.

The Hermit

I want to be alone! A hermit is someone who lives by themselves and apart from the rest of society. Historically, hermits do this for religious reasons to focus on deep thoughts. The Hermit tarot card serves a similar purpose. It's telling you to enjoy a period of self-reflection, so you can find out what it is you need to do to be able to move forwards with confidence. What will help you light your way through the darkness of confusion with renewed clarity?

Upright

Drawing an upright Hermit card is a signal for you to take some time to consider the path you've taken so far in life and where you want to go from this point onwards. The Hermit is a wise character and is telling you to look inwards for the answers and to call on your own wisdom and experience to get the advice you need, rather than asking other people. What is the issue in your life that's not working for you right now? Is it a relationship or job? Taking yourself off for some 'me' time is your chance to reassess. Focus on what needs sorting in your life and work out how to resolve it.

Reversed

A reversed Hermit can mean you are withdrawing from parts of your life too much or overdoing things in some way. It can point to a lack of connection with other people, or being too isolated or cut off from feelings. Or have you exhausted yourself by burning the candle at both ends? These things can leave you tired and filled with anxiety. Embracing The Hermit's state of reflection should be done with care. It doesn't mean adding to the stress by overthinking things. The idea is to clear your mind in order to find clarity and focus. Go for long walks, write down your thoughts and feelings or meditate.

Wheel Of Fortune

The Wheel of Fortune tarot card is a timely reminder that nothing stays the same forever. Like a wheel that keeps on turning, life is constantly changing. Change is an inevitable part of life. It happens whether we're ready for it or not. One of the secrets of living successfully is to learn to accept and handle the changes coming our way, whether we want them or not. After all, isn't that what keeps life fresh and exciting?

Upright

An upright Wheel of Fortune card is a sign that good luck or new opportunities are coming your way. It's your destiny. The wheel is in motion and it's bringing positive change into your life. Get ready to be transformed. Appreciate this moment. Relish your relationships, your world and the luck you've been gifted by the universe. Make the most of the chances you're offered.

The Wheel of Fortune card is also linked to karma. If the change that's turning your way now doesn't feel good, is it karma? If you made bad choices that put negative energy out there, it could be boomeranging back to you. If we put kindness out into the world, kindness is the karma that returns...

Reversed

Reversed Wheel of Fortune cards suggest you are being resistant to change. Refusing to accept change doesn't stop it from happening. It just puts off the inevitable and could ultimately cause negative results. For instance, when we try to avoid change of any kind, we often build up feelings of stress and anxiety. Instead, dig deep and try to discover why change is hard for you. How can you work on these feelings and find a way to accept and respond to destiny's game more positively? Yes, change can be painful, but you need to go with the flow and see where those changes might take you. The end result might be better than you imagine.

Justice

The Justice card is all about fairness, truth and balance. So, if life is feeling unfair and you feel like you're getting the short end of the stick, the Justice card tells you to hang in there. Has someone been lying about you? The truth will come out... eventually. Do you feel someone has wronged you? They won't get away with it. As long as you are behaving honestly and fairly, balance will be restored. It may take longer than you'd like, but justice will prevail.

Upright

The upright Justice card is a reminder to face the music! It's about visualising the potential consequences of the choices we make honestly, not through rose-tinted glasses that only show you what you want them to be. Then, follow this up by doing what you know is right according to your own moral compass and your inner sense of what is right and wrong. This won't always be easy, but it always feels good to act with integrity. And don't forget, justice is all about balance: sending good energy out into the universe also means at some point those good vibes will come right back at you.

Reversed

Drawing a reversed Justice card is a sign we've messed up. Everyone makes mistakes or does something they'd rather not shout about from the rooftops. Don't sweat it. There is always time to make amends. Don't beat yourself up too much. Talk to yourself as you would to a best friend if they were doing their best in a difficult situation and got it wrong. Whatever the rights and wrongs of a problem, the thing that matters most is how you handle it. Accountability is the key word here. 'Fess up and admit your mistakes. Then you can take action to right any wrongs. Don't let pride or shame get in the way of saying sorry and making amends.

The Hanged Man

The Hanged Man tarot card looks like something to run away from – but in fact it's all about hanging around. In a fast-paced world, where more and bigger is always supposed to mean better, the Hanged Man encourages us to stop and let it all hang out! Drawing this card can mean take a break, do nothing. Pause, wait and see what happens and reflect on what is happening in your life and what it is you really want or should do. You'll only be able to get a fresh perspective by giving yourself some space for quiet contemplation.

Upright

Do things feel like they're going pear-shaped? Nothing going your way however hard you try? Drawing an upright Hanging Man is the universe's way of telling you to press pause. Stop trying to force someone's hand, or give up chasing someone for a decision. Let it go. Things don't always go to plan and sometimes you just have to let them work themselves out. And they will do, eventually. It's frustrating when things don't go your way immediately, but if you wait and reflect you might be pleasantly surprised and perhaps even discover an option or opportunity you didn't know was there!

Reverse

A reversed Hanged Man means the opposite to the upright card. It's telling you to stop hanging around! It's time for action. No more excuses. You've had time to reflect and consider and now it's time to accept the change ahead, no matter if you feel a little uncertain or unsure. Feelings of indecision are just holding you back. Sometimes you just have to bite the bullet. Stop putting off the inevitable. Maybe you're the kind of person who never feels totally ready for change, but sometimes you just have to go with it! It may involve sacrifices but it will be worth it in the end.

Death

In movies, the Death tarot card usually tells us a murder or something sinister is about to happen. Forget that misconception. This powerful card is not about people dying. The Death card is not about literal deaths at all, but about endings and losses that all of us have to tackle at some point. It's about letting go, accepting change and moving on. The Death card is there to help you cope with and be empowered by the closing of doors in your life so you can enjoy opening new ones.

Upright

The upright Death card reminds us that while endings can be difficult, life goes on. If you've lost a job or had a bad break-up, you may feel lost and heartbroken, but time will heal. You will find a new job and a new love, even if it that is hard to imagine when you're in the eye of the storm.

The Death card also encourages us to accept and embrace transformations. You have to be able to close one door before opening another. Everyone goes through transformations, and if you find yourself in a situation, job or love affair that is deeply lacking or you have simply outgrown, the best thing you can do is move on.

Reversed

The reversed Death card is about resistance to change. Are you making like an ostrich and sticking your head in the sand, pretending nothing is changing when it already is or should be? Change is an inevitable and glorious part of life. You can't fight it or ignore it. It might seem scary or you might not know how to make the changes you need to make. It's natural to feel a little cautious. But if you accept that the change is necessary, you know what you need to do. Be bold and fight against any resistance you have to change. Change can be good. It can lead you to better jobs, stronger relationships and a happier life.

Temperance

Life is a rollercoaster. It's full of ups and downs and it feels like we're always seeking the next ride. In the world today we're encouraged to be thrill seekers, constantly on the move and wanting something bigger, better or faster. The Temperance card, on the other hand, is all about balance, moderation, patience and avoiding extremes. It's a reminder to slow down and let things play out instead of seething with frustration when things don't go our way immediately.

Upright

An upright Temperance card is a sign that you need to go steady and find some balance in your life. Temperance is about relaxing and making space to learn what we really need. It's about taking time to see a situation from every angle and maybe listening to someone else's thoughts and opinions about it too. Be patient. Weigh up all the options. Instead of bouncing from one extreme to the other, try to find that happy middle ground. It's okay to go slowly and test out different options to find the mix that works best for you.

Reversed

The opposite of temperance is overindulgence, and drawing the reversed Temperance card is a sign you've been overdoing it. Whether you've been bingeing on food, drink or social media, or spending too much of your hard-earned money on clothes, outings or accessories, you know where the problem is. The Temperance card doesn't mean cut out all your guilty pleasures. It is just suggesting you curb that self-destructive impulse to excess. You know deep down it's not really making you happy. Just like buyer's regret can kick in after too much retail therapy drains your savings, overindulgence can leave a hollow feeling that doesn't lead to long-term satisfaction. So, hit the reset button and work out what you need to do to rebalance.

The Devil

The Devil sounds like a dark tarot card that no one in their right mind would ever want to pick. In fact, facing your demons may be just what you need. The Devil card is all about taking a long, hard look at the parts of your life or behaviours that are making you unhappy, and changing them. It might not make for easy viewing as you examine the dark recesses of your soul, such as your lusts, vices, obsessions and desires, but you'll feel all the better for it. Far from dragging you down to the pits of Hell, the Devil card can be your stairway to Heaven!

Upright

If you draw the upright Devil card it is a challenge to explore your dark side. What are your worst habits and choices? Is your self-indulgence limiting your life? Are you giving in to temptations that aren't good for you and which aren't truly bringing you joy? Is fear or doubt building a wall between you and your future? What are you doing that's preventing you from living your best life? The Devil is a reminder to face these demons and make peace with them or banish them. You can change. You can change jobs, friends, lovers and even a negative frame of mind. It's time to let them go and find your freedom.

Reversed

A reversed Devil card encourages you to give in to your dark side! Be bad, even if it is just for one night. Maybe life is feeling a little restricted and confining and you feel like you're doing nothing but work. Or maybe you're being sensible and saving hard for a car or house. A reversed Devil card is telling you to put on those dancing shoes and let rip. Just a little. Just enough to feel alive again. All work and no play makes us feel dull and miserable. So, get out there and mix it up. Have some fun!

Judgement

Sitting in judgement is all about weighing up options and deciding if something is good or bad. The Judgement card often comes along when you have a big decision or a choice to make that will bring big changes or have a lasting effect. The Judgement card puts the power firmly in your hands. You may be at a turning point in your life. Which path should you take? The Judgement card reminds you to slow down and think things through.

Upright

When you draw The Judgement card upright, it is a reminder that you can rise to the challenges life brings. It comes at a time when you have thought about and learnt from your past experiences and you're able to put the past behind you. You've made peace with wrongdoings or regrets, and let go of any guilt or sadness about the past. You've taken responsibility for the life you have led up to this point and you're ready to reinvent yourself. The upright Judgement card also suggests that it may help to talk to people who face a similar dilemma. You could help each other work out what's best or let them guide you and help you.

Reversed

A Judgement card drawn in reverse is a sign that negative thoughts might be preventing you moving forwards. This could take the form of self-doubts or fears about what might or could happen when you make a particular decision. A reverse Judgement card tells you to stop doubting yourself and to have the confidence to take responsibility for your actions. You can be decisive. Take the opportunity to make changes and give yourself space to grow and reinvent yourself. The reversed Judgement card is also a reminder to stop judging yourself and others. Just as you can allow negative thinking to cause self-doubt, negative thinking can make you judge others unfairly too.

The World

You've got the whole world in your hands! The World card is the final card of the Major Arcana and drawing it from the pack is a signal that you've achieved something big or reached an important goal. You should feel on top of the world! There have doubtless been hiccups along the way, challenges to face from outside and from within yourself, doubts and fears you have had to overcome. Whether it's passing a test, learning a new skill, getting a new job or overcoming a fear, enjoy this moment and the feelings of success and accomplishment it brings.

Upright

Stop the world, I want to get off! Sometimes it feels like you're on a giant hamster wheel and you have to keep running from one thing to the next, never stopping. The problem is that if we never take a moment to celebrate a happy ending before setting out on a new beginning, we never get to relish that sense of personal fulfilment or completion that makes all the hard work worthwhile. The upright World card tells us to do just that. Sure, it's great to see new opportunities ahead, but first be in the here and now long enough to celebrate all that you have achieved. Feel that warm glow of pride. Bask in its light!

Reversed

The reversed World card reminds us that just as we should take a moment to celebrate life's little victories, we should also give ourselves time to get over life's bitter disappointments. Some things come to an end before we are ready for them to or when we don't want them to at all. Dumped by a crush? Sacked from a job you were just getting good at? Nothing lasts forever, all things and situations are temporary, and happiness is fleeting. It's right to allow yourself time to grieve for what once was or could have been. This will help you find the closure you need to be able to move forwards again when you're ready.

MINOR ARCANA

The Minor Arcana cards are called 'minor' because they relate to what's happening in your daily life. These cards don't necessarily signify big picture, life changing events. But being 'minor' doesn't mean these cards are not important or that they won't have an important effect on your life. They are minor in the sense that they are about the here and now. They give you an awareness about how the people, tasks, decisions and events in your everyday life are affecting you.

The story in the cards

The Minor Arcana set is made up of 56 cards. There are four suits of 14 cards each.

- The Suit of Wands represents energy, motivation and passion. The Wands cards often appear in tarot readings about life purpose, spirituality and new ideas.

- The Suit of Cups represents feelings, emotions, intuition and creativity. Cups cards often appear in readings about your emotional relationships.

- The Suit of Swords represents thoughts, words and actions. Swords cards often appear in readings about communicating your ideas, making decisions and asserting your power.

- The Suit of Pentacles represents finances, work and material possessions. The Pentacles cards often appear in readings about financial prosperity.

- The 14 cards in the four suits of cards are divided up in a similar way to an ordinary deck of playing cards. Aces are the first card in each suit, followed by cards two through ten, then four face or court cards: Page, Knight, Queen and King.

The Ace of Wands

Lost your spark? Has your get up and go got up and gone? Don't sweat it. The Ace of Wands is the first card of the Minor Arcana and heralds a new beginning for you too. It represents passion and potential and could be just the inspiration and motivation you need to get going on something new. The Ace of Wands is a great card to have up your sleeve (or on your tarot table) but it's not a magic bullet. You need to seize those new opportunities, find your enthusiasm and make your own breakthroughs. This card encourages you to run with any new desire and drive you may have in order to launch yourself on your journey.

Upright

Drawing an upright Ace of Wands should ignite the spark within you and remind you that this is your chance for a new adventure. Now is the time to stop the excuses and hesitation and to set aside the doubts and negativity. If you've been stalling with a plan to follow a career, project or hobby you feel passionate about, now's the time to do it. If you're asking questions about your love life, the upright Ace of Wands also suggests the person you're interested in is more to do with lust and passion than life-long commitment.

Reversed

A reversed Ace of Wands suggests you're struggling to release your potential or creativity. It's here to remind you that self-doubt and negativity can kill creativity and suffocate any motivation you might have. The secret is just to give it a go. A blank canvas or new opportunity can be scary, but don't let fear hold you back. Be patient. Your breakthrough will come. Growth takes time and effort. You'll get there. Just have a little faith and you'll find what inspires you and your new beginning.

Two of Wands

The Ace of Wands heralds new beginnings, and the Two of Wands is about the next steps you take. This card is about flexibility and choice. The image on the card usually shows someone looking out at the world beyond as if they're about to begin a new adventure. The only way to find out what lies ahead is to get out there! Yes, you have some choices and decisions to make, but drawing this card also suggests you are ready to meet the challenges ahead.

Upright

Drawing an upright Two of Wands suggests potential and discovery. It's a card of possibilities and what could be. If you're thinking of going on a trip, do it! Or, maybe you're unhappy at work or in love. What are your options and which path will you take? In the worlds of money and work this card hints at success, but only if you make the right choices and take good advice. This card can also refer to a long-distance relationship, and suggests it might be worth your while travelling and taking a chance. A word of caution, though: if you're going through a rocky time in a relationship, this card doesn't mean bail on it. Rather, take some time to work on the partnership you already have. Try to reignite that spark before giving up on it.

Reversed

A reversed Two of Wands suggests you're feeling restless or fearful. Perhaps you're worried you don't have many options or you're scared of the new and unknown, or perhaps you have been hurt by a sudden change in the past? This card is about the things that hold us back from forging ahead. Try to combat these issues by working out what is stopping you and what causes those feelings. Then find a way to fight those feelings so you can start to step out into the world that you deserve.

Three of Wands

It's time to step up. The Three of Wands is a card that represents growth and progress. It suggests that you have an idea of where you want to go, who you want to be with, or what you want to be, and now it is time to take action. This card is the signal you have been waiting for that it's time to go after that thing you desire. This is your time and you have a lot to look forward to if only you seize the opportunities for progress and growth in front of you!

Upright

This card is all about making your dreams a reality. Do you want to see the world? If you've been fantasising about taking a big trip or heading off on an adventure for a while, then make it happen. Only you can free up the time to go, buy the tickets, and book those rides. If you want to move up the career ladder, maybe you need to get out of your comfort zone and switch companies. Or perhaps you want to take your relationship to the next level? You'll need to work out what exactly you want and talk about this with your loved one to make it happen. Progress and growth take effort and will only happen if you get out there and make them happen.

Reversed

If the upright Three of Wands is all about opportunities, progress, growth and the future, the reversed Three of Wands is more about the limitations, obstacles and delays that prevent you from reaching those goals. No one said change and challenges were easy, but without them we'd all stagnate. Setting self-imposed limits on your life by being scared of what's next or only seeing the risks or downsides isn't helping you. Don't delay and wait around for life to come to you. You've got a plan. Stick to it. It will be worth it in the end.

Four of Wands

Light the candles, crack open the bubbly, gather everyone together for a good time. It is time to party! The Four of Wands is telling you the good times are here. It's a card that represents growth, harmony and celebration. It's about the pleasure and fulfilment that comes with reaching an important goal or achieving a success either personally or as a team or community.

Upright

The Four of Wands upright card is telling you it's time to celebrate and let the good times roll. In terms of love and relationships, it hints that maybe a wedding or commitment ceremony is coming up or perhaps simply that your partnership is destined for bliss. It can also suggest a possible blast from the past; perhaps a reunion with an old flame? At work it can mean your team has finished a project or reached a milestone. As a card linked with home and family, it's also about celebrating surprises, festive times, birthdays, homecomings or reunions with those you love most. It's about feeling supported and secure as you come together with your family or community or team. It's time to pause, relax and celebrate what you have achieved so far.

Reversed

The Four of Wands reversed can mean the celebration is more personal than shared. Perhaps you've managed that marathon after months of training or learnt a new skill. It's not necessarily something that you feel the need to broadcast to the world, but you should take time to celebrate your own personal achievements too. Or perhaps you've reached a new level of self-assurance and satisfaction in your life. That's a reason to rejoice as well.

On the other hand, a reversed Four of Wands could mean there's trouble in your family or home or conflict with others. Or perhaps it signals a time of transition, some upheavals at work or perhaps it's time to move house and make a new home. The reversed Four of Wands is a warning to sort out tension and communication problems as soon as they happen, or that party may never come about!

Five of Wands

When people hear The Five of Wands tarot card is about competition, conflict and rivalry, they often think it's a negative card. Far from it. This card is about the opportunities for growth that come when you face challenges or when you are in conflict or competition with others. The Five of Wands is a positive and active card that's telling you to commit and focus.

Upright

Feels like you're hitting your head against a brick wall? The Five of Wands upright suggests that conflict or competition with others is holding you back. This could be in work, sports or even sexual play. When facing a challenge like this, hit pause and focus on finding a resolution. Listen to other people's opinions, even if you don't agree with them. You might learn something and if you listen to them, they'll listen to you. Rivalry can make people strive to be better and conflict can result in new solutions to problems. If you can work with other people and navigate the choppy waters of confrontation, you'll bond as a group and be able to make the best of all the ideas and talent around.

Reversed

The reversed Five of Wands can suggest you're giving up, running scared, or just doing enough to get the job done. Where's the satisfaction in that? It can suggest you avoid conflict even when it could be a useful thing. There's no hiding anymore. This card is telling you it's time to go all in and commit with total focus and discipline. That's the only way to beat the competition.

This reversed card can also indicate that you have internal conflicts. Maybe you're not sure where you stand on some important topics and find you're easily swayed by other people. Or maybe you're battling with a decision about leaving a job or relationship. The only way you're going to find harmony is by resolving the problems. Have those discussions and arguments, however uncomfortable they are. You'll feel better for it.

Six of Wands

Good for you! Drawing a Six of Wands tarot card indicates success and personal achievement. Perhaps you just got a promotion, award, finished a tricky project or won a tough argument? Or maybe you've achieved a personal goal? This card is here to tell you to enjoy your success. You have worked hard and deserve the recognition you're getting.

Upright

The Six of Wands upright indicates you have been working on your goals and achievements and you've come to a point where you can reap the benefits. If you're single, your confidence is attractive and it could mean someone special is waiting for you to make a move. If you're in a relationship and you're working towards something, like moving in together, it's time to make those plans a reality. Healthwise you should be feeling strong and healthy, and if you're unwell you should feel better soon. Your hard work has shown up in your bank account and in your job and you should be feeling flush and getting good reviews at work. Enjoy your moment, but don't let it go to your head. Stay humble. No one wants to hear you bragging.

Reversed

Perhaps things are not going your way in love, life work or finances? Drawing a Six of Wands reversed can mean you're lacking confidence or doubting your decisions or abilities. Perhaps you're anxious about letting people down. Sometimes a lack of motivation can happen when you don't feel you're getting the recognition you deserve, or maybe your bank account or career has taken a hit. Don't lose sight of your own feelings and desires and just do what other people want or tell you. The reversed card can suggest someone is looking to stab you in the back, so this is not the time to be easily swayed. Keep trusted friends and family close. They'll help you rebuild that self-belief.

Seven of Wands

Everyone loves a winner, right? Sadly that's not always the case. When you're successful in life and things are going well, there is always someone who will try to bring you down. There could well be an increase in 'haters', trolls, or people who want what you have. The Seven of Wands is your cosmic reminder to have strength in the face of competition and to protect what you've worked so hard to achieve.

Upright

The upright Seven of Wands is telling you to stay true to yourself and follow your heart. You know what is right so make sure you stand up for yourself and others. This can mean expressing yourself through your work, but it also means speaking up against injustice. This could mean joining a campaign or cause that is important to you, or speaking up to defend someone or something in your daily life. You are in a good place, so use that confidence and success to advocate for others. Protect their rights. If someone is trying to pull you down, take the high road and focus instead on doing something that you believe in to help others.

Reversed

The reversed Seven of Wands can mean the haters are winning. Do you feel their negativity and criticism wearing you down? There will always be someone trying to pull you down, especially when you are someone who is true to themselves and speaking up or doing something interesting. That's no reason to hide or go back into your shell. You can't please everyone all of the time. Taking a stance means there will always be someone on the other side. Don't let them dampen your self-belief. Who cares what they think? Leave them whining in the background while you get on and do your thing.

Eight of Wands

It's time to throw yourself into the future. The Eight of Wands card is all about action and forward momentum. So dive on in, the water's lovely! Don't waste precious time. This card is all about feeling the energy and bursting into life. It's a signal for you to be assertive and get things done. Don't just plan it, do it!

Upright

Busy, busy, busy. The Eight of Wands upright encourages you to move ahead with enthusiasm and energy. Don't fight change. Go with it. It might feel like things are moving a little too fast, but don't miss this chance to follow your goals and dreams. The stars are in alignment, so focus all of your attention and efforts on your goals. Ditch distractions and focus on the job in hand. If you concentrate and you're truly determined, you can activate those plans or those changes you want. It might also mean packing your bags! The fast-paced movement linked to this card upright can also suggest it's time for a trip, whether that's for business or pleasure.

Reversed

The Eight of Wands reversed can mean that you're rushing ahead with a plan that's only half-baked. It's a warning from the cosmos to take your foot off the pedal while you think through your options more carefully. Or, it may mean you need to stay focused in a more mindful way on the job in hand. Don't be distracted by things that stop you from reaching your goal.

The Eight of Wands reversed can also be cautioning you against being resistant to change. If you're stuck in a rut, try to mix things up a bit to find your positive energy so you can start moving forwards again. This forward movement can be literal too. Perhaps you're experiencing delays or obstacles stopping you from moving ahead with travel or other plans. That's frustrating. Once the situation is right, you'll know it and can kick-start progress again.

Nine of Wands

You've got this! Like the best friend who's got your back, The Nine of Wands is here to reassure you that you can handle whatever comes your way. This card represents courage, protection and resilience. It's a sign that you're prepared for the battles that lie ahead, so don't even think about giving up on those big plans you've made for the future.

Upright

The upright Nine of Wands is telling you that you have put in the time on yourself and your life and you are ready to face the challenges ahead. You have the persistence and resilience to work through your exhaustion or challenges. You're so close to success you can smell it, so don't stop now.

In the world of love, the upright Nine of Wands is a sign that to get the relationship you want might take work on both sides and some sacrifices. Love isn't easy, but it's worth it. This card can also suggest money worries or feeling tired or stressed at work. Show some true grit and hang on in there. Persistence will pay off.

Reversed

The Nine of Wands reversed suggests you don't feel you have what it takes to make a big or long-term change. Maybe you don't think of yourself as a risk-taker or you're worried about being trapped in a situation that doesn't work out. Perhaps you find it hard to really open up to people or trust them. This has to change if you're going to grow and get what you want. Fortune favours the brave. Just think carefully about the decisions you make before going ahead.

In relationships, perhaps your love life is stalling or one person is putting in more effort than the other. In work, you might be struggling or feeling burnt-out or perhaps money woes are dragging you down. The reversed card is warning you to deal with whatever the problems are because these are preventing you from moving onwards.

Ten of Wands

Do you feel like you're weighed down by a heavy load right now? The Ten of Wands symbolises hard work and burnout. It suggests you may be feeling overwhelmed and have too much on your plate. The Ten of Wands is here to tell you it's time to offload some of that stuff you don't really need to do or to get some help unburdening yourself of the emotional weight that's pressing down on you.

Upright

An upright Ten of Wands means taking on extra responsibilities in different ways. Sometimes it's a good and temporary kind of extra workload. Perhaps you're providing a friend with a shoulder to cry on or vent to, putting in extra hours to earn enough money to pay for something you really need, or caring for a poorly parent. These extra responsibilities add to your load, but they are short-term and you know they're the right things to do.

The Ten of Wands upright may also be drawn when things have built up gradually and you're now worn out. It's a cosmic reminder to work out what's really urgent and set some boundaries. Make sure you get some rest and relaxation too. It's good to work hard to reach your goals, but keep some fuel in the tank to enjoy your success when you get there.

Reversed

A reversed Ten of Wands card suggests you're a lone ranger, taking on too much for yourself. Get a grip. Share some of the responsibilities and duties and don't take on any more. You're heading for burnout and if you don't make a change you won't be able to do any of it. Whether it's a heavy workload, emotional hurt or family responsibility, it's good to share. Only by talking about it or asking for help will you find relief. You may be surprised by how good it feels to receive help from people who care about you too.

Page of Wands

Ready for an adventure? The Page of Wands card represents discovery, inspiration and a youthful spirit. This card suggests you're in a big, bold phase of growth and experimentation, exploring what it is you want to do next. Feeling inspired? Go with it! See where those big ideas take you. Let your curiosity and excitement lead you to some new experiences and escapades.

Upright

The Page of Wands upright is telling you to follow your impulses and enthusiasms. Channel that enthusiasm into anything that comes your way. Let your curiosity for the new be your guide. Say yes to those impulses and opportunities, whether that means a new hobby, new style, new crush or even an exciting trip or new career. It doesn't matter that you don't know how things are going to turn out. How boring would that be anyway? If you have a bright idea, this is the time to run with it. Call on your inner daredevil to give you the courage to take a chance and see what happens next.

Reversed

A reversed Page of Wands may be a wake-up call. While it's great to try new directions, you won't get very far if you keep straying from the path! It takes effort to embark on a new adventure. You can't get off the bus before it reaches its destination, or you'll never find out what's there. So, stay with it and even when that first wave of excitement about a new idea or endeavour flatlines, keep going. That might mean putting in some hours or tweaking ideas to improve them. Relationships, jobs and skills all require a little effort and fine-tuning. Don't let fears and anxieties dampen your enthusiasm. Keep asking questions and at some point you'll find the answer you've been looking for.

Knight of Wands

Are you feeling up for anything and ready to take on the world? The Knight of Wands is a card fired up with inspiration, passion and impulsivity. It suggests you are ready for action and keen to charge ahead. You know what you want, and you have the energy and enthusiasm to make it happen. The Knight of Wands is here to tell you it's time to gallop into your future.

Upright

Drawing the upright Knight of Wands card means you are glowing with confidence and ready to face any obstacles in your way as you pursue your goals, whether that be in love, your career, your finances or whatever. You laugh in the face of danger because you know the rewards that await you. Your new confidence and enthusiasm are very attractive, so don't be surprised if you get some extra attention too.

But beware. Don't let confidence make you reckless. Don't let that burst of energy make you impulsive and impatient. If you rush headfirst into things without any thought you'll make mistakes. Channel that energy and enthusiasm into thoughts first and deeds later. Think through your options and make the right moves at the right time. Then, go for it!

Reversed

The Knight of Wands reversed can indicate you're fired up by a project that is particularly personal to you. It's not about chasing fame or money, but about your own sense of pleasure and satisfaction. Enjoy the chance to do something that sparks your joy, whatever it is.

The Knight of Wands reversed can also suggest that you're not sure how to channel your energy and enthusiasm. Something is holding you back or someone is getting in your way. Try to find a different way to reach your goal.

Yet another reading is that the reversed Knight of Wands is warning you to slow down and take your time. Don't act impulsively or rush things. You don't need to do it all at once. Give yourself time to work out what's best.

Queen of Wands

The Queen of Wands is a cosmic reminder to be your most energetic, ambitious and dynamic self. This card represents confidence, inspiration and encouragement. The Queen of Wands is a leader and her card is telling you to be fearless and assertive too. You've achieved a lot of growth and success and you need to keep that momentum. Take pride in your accomplishments and bring others along for the ride.

Upright

An upright Queen of Wands suggests you are a brave, positive and independent person who knows how to make the best of their strengths and achieve their goals. There may be some roadblocks along the way, but you know how to inspire others to help you get where you're going. Trust your instincts and believe in your self-worth. Stay focused on your plans and don't be afraid to go after what you want, just don't step on anyone else's toes as you climb that ladder.

Your energy and enthusiasm radiate positivity and you can be an inspiration to others. You are a bit of a social butterfly and enjoy fluttering around a room, sharing your charm and spreading the love. Use that influence to meet new people or form a group to do great things.

Reversed

The Queen of Wands reversed shows you know yourself well. You have worked out who you are and what you stand for and this has given you high self-esteem and a deep level of confidence.

This card can also suggest that maybe you're feeling a little more reserved and withdrawn than usual. The party animal has been replaced by the wallflower. Lean into it. Be how you feel. Maybe some alone time is what you need right now. That will give you a chance to re-establish that sense of self you have deep down. Don't let others influence you. Listen to yourself and rely on your own strengths and talents.

King of Wands

The King of Wands is a card about leadership and skill. It represents the people in life who make a difference: the teachers, coaches, mentors, bosses, elders or entrepreneurs who solve problems and make changes. They have a clear purpose and are able to view problems from all angles to help them come up with cutting-edge solutions. The King of Wands card encourages you to step up and trust yourself to be a leader too.

Upright

Drawing a King of Wands tarot card upright, is a heavy hint that it's time for you to take the wheel! You may have ideas, skills, talents and a clear plan, but the only way you're going to make that plan into a reality is to get other people onside to help you. You have a vision, now be a visionary. Entrepreneurs don't wait for chances, they follow their passions and stay focused until their goals are accomplished. If you need some inspiration or help, think about who inspires you and who you can learn from. Ask them to mentor you or have a conversation with them about how to proceed and engage your inner king!

Reversed

Being a leader often means being confident, loud and dominant in order to get your ideas heard and persuade people to follow you. However, if you draw the reversed King of Wands, it could be suggesting your confidence has turned to arrogance and your single-mindedness has become a negative. Have you become egotistical and conceited and too convinced of your own invincibility? If your head gets too swollen, and you start to believe your own hype that bit too much, you'll make mistakes. Good leaders listen to other people's ideas and encourage others to take part. Working with other people and being open to feedback and other opinions is the real hallmark of a great leader.

Ace of Cups

Love is all you need... or so the song goes, and the Ace of Cups card is all about love. It's about giving love to yourself and others and being open to receiving love from yourself and others. It's about the flow of love from within. It's a signal to follow your feelings and trust your heart rather than your head. The Ace of Cups is all about understanding and expressing your own emotions and being open to greater intimacy, deeper connections, and long-lasting, truly satisfying relationships.

Upright

An upright Ace of Cups points to new love. If you're unattached, it could mean a new relationship is about to blossom. This could be a new romantic relationship, a new friendship or something else. If there is someone you're interested in, then this is the time to open your heart and tell them how you feel. Go on, ask them for their number or a date! If you're already in a relationship, this card could indicate it's time to get closer to the other person. Tell them how much you care and what future you see together. Write a poem or a love letter or send flowers or a gift. Go big or go home. The path to true happiness and contentment lies ahead.

Reversed

A reversed Ace of Cups might suggest it's time for some self-love. Prioritise yourself and your own wellbeing and self-esteem. What's holding you back from accepting and loving who you are? Once you feel comfortable in your own skin and have learnt to love yourself, you're more likely to find that special someone too.

The Ace of Cups reversed can also be telling you to drop your guard. Perhaps the reason you're not getting the love you deserve is that you won't let anyone in. It's scary to let people get really close. What if you get hurt? The rewards are too great not to take the chance. Of course, if you've been deeply hurt it may just mean you need a little more time for those wounds to heal before getting out there again. That's okay too.

Two of Cups

It takes two, baby! The Two of Cups card is an expression of the current of love that flows between two people. This card is a signal that a relationship you're in or are soon going to have is one of true and deep connection. It's possible that this partnership could evolve into something deeply satisfying and rewarding and perhaps last a long time.

Upright

Drawing an upright Two of Cups card indicates you could be about to embark on a new partnership. This doesn't necessarily mean a new lover or life partner, it could also be a business partner or close friend. The good news is that this new union is one based on mutual attraction and understanding. It will be a relationship that's good for both of you and is an equally shared affection. In some cases, the Two of Cups can even suggest a marriage, proposal or engagement is on the cards.

In business, the upright Two of Cups tells you what you probably already know: the partner or colleague you're working closely with is a great fit. Your skills complement each other and you trust and respect each other. Good communication should mean this lasts.

Reversed

The reversed Two of Cups reminds you of the importance of self-love. If you feel you're deserving of love, you'll have better relationships with other people – and yourself! You'll be comfortable in your own skin and able to be yourself. The Two of Cups reversed can suggest you don't have enough self-esteem. This can make you too needy and demanding or jealous and this makes you vulnerable to hurt. So, dig deep and find the self-love you need and deserve.

The Two of Cups reversed can also indicate a break-up or some disharmony or distrust in a relationship. To get past the issues that are damaging your relationship, you need to talk. Say how you feel, listen to what the other person has to say. Find your way through the gloom together.

Three of Cups

It's time to dig out those dancing shoes! The Three of Cups is a card of togetherness, celebration and friendship. This card is a sign that you have something to celebrate, from finalising a creative project to starting a new adventure. It tells you happiness is coming your way, and it's the kind of contentment that will endure and that you can share with the people you care about. Celebrate with your friends and family and relish their companionship and support.

Upright

The upright Three of Cups urges you to get together with your best buddies. These are the people you can count on. You support each other through life's ups and downs. Take the time to talk, laugh and share news and ideas with each other. This card is your invitation to party. It suggests you have a busy social life on the horizon, so make the most of it and enjoy some good times.

When upright, this card is also a reminder you can do great things together when you collaborate with people on a creative project. Working with like-minded people on a shared project feels great and does you good, whether that's in an art club or on a community project.

Reversed

The reversed Three of Cups card indicates you'd rather fly solo for now. Perhaps you've been partying too hard and you just need some rest. Or perhaps things aren't gelling in your friendship group and you need some distance from it. Maybe a spell of independence and freedom from the crowds will be nurturing and give you the chance to work out who you really like and want to be with.

In terms of work, this card can suggest you work independently rather than in a group, to avoid your personal creativity or ideas bring squashed by others. If you're feeling stressed and burnt-out, it can also mean you need some time off work. Try to leave work worries at home and see friends and family instead to benefit from their love and support.

Four of Cups

Feeling meh? Same old, same old? The Four of Cups card symbolises negativity and introspection. It suggests you're feeling a bit pessimistic and glass-half-empty. Perhaps you're feeling a bit run down and lacking in energy and enthusiasm and turning inward on yourself, getting bogged down in your own gloom and doom. This Four of Cups card is here to remind you to cast off that negativity and cynicism and amend your attitude.

Upright

Drawing the Four of Cups upright indicates you're looking at life through the opposite of rose-tinted glasses. All you can see right now are the worst case scenarios. It feels like your plug has been pulled and you're running on zero motivation. It's also a caution not to allow your negativity, sorrow or guilt to lead to lost chances. Don't let your lack of mojo make you turn down opportunities that could lead to good things. Saying no might be the right choice, but think your options through before dismissing them. Take time to assess what's best.

Reversed

A reversed Four of Cups card suggests that perhaps a bit of alone time is what you need. Retreating into your nest and taking some 'me' time could be your chance to focus on your needs. Just try not to cut out all contact with friends and family. Simply explain this is a temporary situation and you'll be in touch again soon.

It can also mean that a period of self-isolation has done the trick and you're ready to get back out there with renewed enthusiasm. Time alone and some self-reflection has given you the chance to heal and reassess your situation. It's helped you to grow and get back out there and start making some changes.

Five of Cups

Grab a tissue. This card is a bit of a downer. The Five of Cups is all about loss, regret and sadness. While there are new opportunities and potential out there, all you can see right now are your disappointments and failures. Fixating on your losses is preventing you from taking the opportunities available to you. While it represents negativity, this card is also a reminder that even though you feel downhearted and lost at this minute, it is always possible to move on and start again.

Upright

When an upright Five of Cups appears, it suggests you're upset and disappointed because something hasn't turned out the way you wanted or expected it too. Failure and regret are weighing heavy on you and you're finding it hard not to sink into self-pity. Or perhaps you're finding it hard to let go of past disappointments. Sure, you need time to feel your pain, but don't dwell too long before moving on. You may need to forgive yourself or for others to forgive you. Everyone makes mistakes. The important thing is to learn from them and move on to the new opportunities and possibilities that are waiting for you. Ditch the pessimism and regrets and try to be more positive and optimistic.

Reversed

The reversed Five of Cups is a sign that you feel you've let yourself or others down and that you're to blame for a setback. Don't hide your pain. Talking to others about how you feel will bring relief and comfort. They will help you to forgive yourself and move on. You can't change what happened in the past, but you can appreciate that pain can mean gain. If you work out what's wrong, you can learn from past experiences and be open to new opportunities even if there is a risk you could be hurt again.

—◆◆◆—

Six of Cups

The Six of Cups is the tarot card equivalent of a warm cup of hot chocolate, a fluffy blanket and your favourite childhood film. It's about nostalgia and basking in the warm glow of past memories of simpler, happy times. So, put on those rose-tinted glasses and enjoy the show. Nostalgia is comforting and it's a reminder of what makes you, you! It gives you hope when the world around you feels like it is going mad.

Upright

Drawing an upright Six of Cups is your cue to look to your past for some help appreciating the present. What made you feel good when you were younger and things felt easier? Are there hobbies, activities or even sounds that can enhance your life in the here and now? This could be as simple as listening to tunes from your past or making time to do some sketching or colouring like you used to do. Perhaps you're struggling in the present because you've fallen out with a friend, had a bad break-up or you're just feeling lost. Indulging in some childhood memories and nostalgia can help you reconnect with yourself and rediscover some of your earlier joy and energy.

Reversed

Are you in danger of being stuck in the past? The reversed Six of Cups might be telling you to stop looking at the past so indulgently. Nothing is perfect and it's a mistake to put memories up on a pedestal and only remember the good stuff. This can really cause problems, especially if you forget the parts of a friendship or relationship that were bad for you or the reasons you left that job in the first place. It's good to enjoy past memories, but it's not good to lose yourself in the past. There's plenty of fun to be had in the present.

Seven of Cups

Opportunity knocks! The Seven of Cups card is here to tell you there are a lot of opportunities, choices and options out there waiting for you. Just make sure you make the right choices and decisions about which ones to take. Don't pick the first, shiniest option you see. Pick the one that really will be best for you in the real world. Watch out for illusions. Look at circumstances, opportunities and people for what they really are, rather than what you want them to be.

Upright

The upright Seven of Cups is a cosmic reality check. Do you spend more time on wishful thinking and fantasies than reality? It's fun to imagine all the options and opportunities out there waiting for you to choose from, but temper this with a dose of realism too. And don't let wishful thinking stop you from enjoying what you already have!

Good things are not just going to fall into your lap. Do something to help make your dreams into reality. But do so with open eyes. Nothing is perfect and there are downsides to everything. Think about what you can do to make the changes you want in your life. It won't get you there immediately, but it will feel good to be doing something about it.

Reversed

The Seven of Cups reversed card is here to tell you to wake up and smell the coffee. Life isn't something you should just allow to drift. It's time to start making things happen. Take a long, hard look at what you want and why you're not getting out there and making it happen. Then make a plan for what to do next.

The reversed card is also a reminder to analyse what you really want, and not get distracted by what other people think you should do. It can be tough to make changes and choices, but you can do it. Brainstorm your options. Make a list of what you don't want. Then list the pros and cons of the stuff you do want. You can do this.

Eight of Cups

Sometimes you just need to let it go. The Eight of Cups is telling you not to be afraid to let go and move on if something isn't working out as you'd hoped. It's a red light telling you to stop and consider if this thing is worth all your precious time and effort. Or is it simply time to walk out the door? This isn't as negative as it sounds. The Eight of Cups is about abandoning a bad situation or lost cause, not about abandoning hope. By walking away, you allow yourself to move on and make the transition to something new and better.

Upright

We all get trapped by the impulse to stay in a job, relationship or situation because it's familiar, was once great, or we've already put so much time and effort in to make it work. The upright Eight of Cups card is here to tell you that once something isn't working, it is better to walk away. It's time for some home truths. This thing isn't right for you anymore and won't go back to what it once was. You're wasting your time and you risk missing out on future fun. It's time to move on. It's time to admit defeat and start getting excited about what comes next.

Reversed

The reversed Eight of Cups card suggests you take time to work out what your next move is. Perhaps the relationship, work or other situation isn't a lost cause. Is it really over? Could it be worth trying to salvage what was there? Have you really done all you can to make it work? If you walk away now, can you be sure you really gave it a go, honestly? Think long and hard about your situation as it really is and don't let other people sway your decision. If you decide to move on, you want to be sure you'll have no regrets and that you know it was the correct move to make.

Nine of Cups

Like the fairy godmother who drops in to bring happiness to a fairy tale, the Nine of Cups card is here to grant your wishes! This card is all about emotional fulfilment, satisfaction and contentment. You feel blessed and there's an extra spring in your step as you go about your daily life because you feel like things are going your way.

Upright

Drawing an upright Nine of Cups is a sign that life is treating you well. Your work, relationships, health and social life are everything you wished for. Everything seems to be falling into place for you, so enjoy it! Make the most of the good times when they happen. Just remember to be thankful for what you have. Take stock of all the things you're grateful for so that you appreciate them. If you're still waiting for that upturn, being grateful for what you do have always helps too. Live in the moment, because everything is temporary and the good times may not keep on rolling.

Reversed

A reversed Nine of Cups card suggests that a dark cloud is threatening to block out your sunshine. Is there something that is spoiling your chances of enjoying what happiness you have? Is work going brilliantly, but friendships are faltering? Do you have money but no time or a lack of love? Or have you been overindulging and overspending and found that it just leaves you feeling empty? Inner happiness doesn't come from material wealth. The reversed Nine of Cups indicates you should work out what really matters to you and what will make you happy instead of chasing success.

This card can also suggest a dissatisfaction with life and your current situation. If things aren't working out, try going at things from a different angle to reach your goals.

Ten of Cups

Happy days. The Ten of Cups card is an expression of happy relationships, joy and contentment. It's a card that suggests the stars are in alignment and there is a bounty of bliss ahead. Love and happiness are in the air, and it's time to surround ourselves with the warmth and affection of friends, family, and loved ones. This card is about the enriching love that people share and the way they lift up and support each other. It also conveys the deep pleasure it brings us all to see those we care about being happy and fulfilled as well.

Upright

The Ten of Cups upright card signifies that you are enjoying a period of family harmony, when everyone is getting along and you're enjoying each other's company. It feels good. Make the most of this moment and the way it is forging stronger bonds between you all. In terms of love interests, this upright card can suggest a new relationship is going to blossom or perhaps an existing one is going to move to the next level. Follow your heart and when something feels right, go with it. You can trust your instincts at the moment.

Reversed

A reversed Ten of Cups points to you feeling isolated from friends, family, or other loved ones. Things may just seem off. Your values don't seem to align or your lines of communication are down. Ask yourself if your idea of the relationship is unrealistic. Every relationship has its problems sometimes. Can you find a way of making it work and reach a better understanding? If you really try and the relationship is still struggling, maybe it is time to move on.

This card can also suggest that you're not being true to yourself and that you're allowing other people to tell you what you need. You should work out what you want if you are going to really commit to what you're doing. A better balance between work and your personal life can give you the contentment and happiness you deserve.

Page of Cups

It's playtime, people! The Page of Cups is about being curious, idealistic, and fun-loving. Open your mind to all the options out there and you might unearth surprising new aspects of life and yourself. This card is about unleashing your creative potential and following your dreams, however wild they may be. The Page of Cups is telling you to let loose your inner child and reconnect with your inner joy.

Upright

An upright Page of Cups card points to a new idea or creative opportunity coming your way. Seize this moment and have some fun with it. Whether that means taking a pottery class, learning to play an instrument, or working on your tarot card reading, express yourself! Be curious. Play around with new ideas and see where they lead. Trust your intuition. If the universe seems to be telling you to follow a dream, give it a go.

The Page of Cups upright can also suggest a good surprise is coming. This surprise could be the arrival of a new crush, the offer of a new job, a chance to try something new or even an announcement of a birth, engagement or marriage.

Reversed

The reversed Page of Cups suggests that you are holding back your creativity in some way. Perhaps you're not ready to share your ideas or progress yet. Or you doubt whether it's good enough. Perhaps you don't know how to turn your ideas into reality. Have the faith of a child and just give it a go and have some fun with it, regardless of the outcome.

At times, the reversed Page of Cups might be telling you that you or someone you know is a little emotionally immature. Maybe you or they are a bit insecure and prone to temper tantrums when things don't go their way. Like Peter Pan, this person doesn't actually want to grow up and face the responsibilities of the real world. It's time they grew up, and if you find you're with someone like this – ditch the babysitting job, you can do better.

Knight of Cups

Do you sometimes wonder if you're in love with the idea of being in love? Then this is the card for you. The Knight of Cups is a card connected to romance, beauty and creativity. It's about being in touch with your feelings, intuition and emotions and being kind and caring to others. This card tells you to have an open heart and share love and emotional warmth freely.

Upright

An upright Knight of Cups card represents love, beauty and creativity. It's showing that you're ready to explore your passions and your dreams, whether that means starting a new hobby or acting as a mediator between warring friends or family members to restore peace and harmony. Follow your intuition and trust it to tell you which direction to take. Like the Knight of Cups, it's okay to allow yourself to be ruled by your heart when making decisions right now. Use your imagination to help you decide what to do in a situation, whether that's in love, business or your daily life. Let your intuition guide you.

Reversed

A reversed Knight of Cups card suggests you're stalling on a creative project rather than taking action. Maybe you're being unrealistic about what it'll take and feeling a bit moody or maybe jealous that others seem to get the opportunities you don't. It's time to stop imagining what it will be like and get real. Work out the logistics involved and only go ahead when you know what you need to do.

The Knight of Cups reversed can also be a warning that you have unrealistic expectations about life in general. You're setting yourself up for disappointment if you rush ahead with plans because they sound new and exciting without really thinking through how they would work for real.

Queen of Cups

How are you doing? Lost your way a little? The Queen of Cups card is all about compassion and nurture, and it can be a reminder to do some self-care and to treat ourselves with the kindness and understanding that will help you find your compass again. When things feel like they're spiralling out of control, the Queen of Cups also prompts us to trust our intuition when making decisions or choices about people, situations and taking chances.

Upright

An upright Queen of Cups card reminds us of the value of unconditional love and really listening to people's needs. This card says you could be be this caring and compassionate too. Use this positive energy to really connect with the people around you at a deeper level, and offer them a shoulder to cry on if that's what they need.

In saying that, don't forget to love yourself. Helping the friends and family who need you is hugely important and satisfying, but don't let your compassionate nature overwhelm you. Absorbing negative energy may help others but don't do this too much or you'll end up hurting yourself.

Reversed

A reversed Queen of Cups shows up when you've overdone the compassion and neglected yourself. You're a sensitive soul and taking on everyone else's emotional burdens can weigh heavy on you. It's time for some self-care. Lean on other people if you need to. Have a bubble bath and relax. You'll be no good to other people if you crash and burn.

This reversed card also appears if you're not being true to your heart and ignoring your instincts. It's a reminder to trust your intuition. That tight feeling in your chest or stomach is there for a reason. It's telling you something feels off. So, listen to your body and do what your instincts tell you to.

King of Cups

The King of Cups is the CEO of emotions. This card oozes calmness. It's all about having the confidence in your ability to handle whatever hurdles lie ahead. It's not about having bragging rights. This card is about quiet confidence and about trusting your instincts, whilst also listening to the voice of reason in your head. That's what helps us all find calm amongst the chaos.

Upright

Drawing an upright King of Cups is the cosmos telling you to relax and stop worrying about the things you cannot change. Try to find your calmness and a balance between your head and your heart. What are your emotions telling you to do and how does this align with what your brain makes of the situation? Work out your best course of action and take your time doing so. Be patient and don't get frustrated if you can't leap to a conclusion quickly. Listening to your heart is a good thing but you also need to assess what is happening rather than acting on a whim. Have faith in your emotional maturity and believe that you can handle the challenges that come your way.

Reversed

A King card can point to someone we already know or a person we are about to meet. A reversed King of Cups card can be a warning that someone insensitive and immature is on your radar. This person doesn't care who they hurt as they go about doing whatever they want in the moment. This person can be trouble, so watch out.

The reversed King of Cups can also suggest you're feeling overburdened or stressed out and holding in those feelings. Trying to ignore or suppress the stress won't get rid of it. Quite the opposite! Let those feelings breathe and work out how to deal with them and how to make things easier for yourself. And don't be shy of asking for help if you need it.

Ace of Swords

Have you been feeling like you can't see the wood for the trees? Or are you feeling confused and unsure of what to do or how to feel? Never fear! The Ace of Swords is here to slice through the fog in your mind and bring fresh clarity to your world. This card is a sign that a breakthrough is coming. It is a cosmic reminder you've got all the tools you need to work out what you must do and where you must go next to escape this fog.

Upright

Drawing an upright Ace of Swords tells you it's time to really knuckle down and find some clarity in a situation. It's time to look at the circumstances from all perspectives and with searing honesty. Don't shy away from examining the negatives as well as the positives. The only way to learn what is best and to reach a breakthrough is by looking at how things really are. Yes, that might mean coming to the conclusion that it's time to cut someone or something out of your life, but your newfound clarity will let you know if that's the right thing to do, even if it's hard.

An Ace of Swords upright is also about speaking your truth and direct, honest communication. Think about or make notes about what you want to say first, and then speak your truth honestly.

Reversed

A reversed Ace of Swords suggests your situation really is tricky. You may be feeling really conflicted and at a loss as to how to proceed and make things better. Whichever way you turn, nothing seems to make any sense. The Ace of Swords reversed is a reminder to break a problem down into more manageable pieces, then find out what you can do to start climbing your way up out of this particular hole you find yourself in.

Two of Swords

It's crunch time, people! The Two of Swords card is a sign that you have a decision to make. But don't panic. This card also reminds you that you have all the answers you need at your fingertips! Just find a way to shut out all the white noise in your life and hear your own inner voice. The world can be a distracting place and other people can be persuasive, but if you find some peace and quiet and listen to your own feelings and wisdom, you'll get the answers you need.

Upright

An upright Two of Swords card can suggest you need to get some perspective on a relationship in your life. Think about what is causing a problem from the other person's point of view and trust your feelings to help you work out what action to take. The advice is similar for your finances or career or even if you want to know about a challenge you face. If you've been sticking to one game plan or following the advice of just one person, now's the time to look at things from other angles and to look inward for some insight into the subject.

Reverse

Drawing the Two of Swords card in reverse can suggest you're feeling lonely and a bit disconnected from a loved one or loved ones right now. Try to trust that you do have the support of friends and family who care about you. Letting go of the need to always be right might also help you achieve better connections with folk.

A reversed Two of Swords can also indicate you should take some time to consider the career or promotion path you've chosen, or what to do about a challenge that lies ahead. Take a moment to breathe, think about what's right for you and trust yourself. You know deep down what you need to do.

Three of Swords

There is no easy way to say this. The message the Three of Swords brings is one of heartbreak, sadness, loss and grief. Your heart is wounded and maybe your body is hurting too. Someone or something has caused you real pain. But take heart. This card also reminds you of your resilience and ability to mend. The pain and hurt will pass and your heart will heal.

Upright

When the Three of Swords is drawn upright it is a sign that you're suffering heartbreak or some kind of deep emotional pain. Perhaps this sorrow has also hit you like a lightning bolt from out of the blue, making it even more devastating. This card reminds you to let that pain out. Cry, yell, punch a pillow. Release your pain. Try not to believe the mean things someone might have said to you, but if you made a mistake, own and learn from it. Always keep looking ahead and focus on feeling better.

Try to remember that grief, pain and loss are a part of life. It's miserable to be in the depths of despair, but pain also plays an important role in making us who we are. Hold on to the fact that sadness, like everything else in life, is temporary and the grief will pass.

Reversed

The Three of Swords reversed encourages you to ditch the negative self-talk and self-criticism. You'd never say those things to a loved one! Focus on the positives. If there is a trait in your personality that needs work, deal with it. Forgive yourself and be the person you know you can be.

This card reversed can also suggest you've lost someone or a relationship has ended, but that you have released that pain and you're feeling more optimistic. Conversely, it can also mean you're struggling to move forwards after such a loss. You have no choice but to accept the pain and the change and find a way to move on. Maybe one way to do this is to forgive either yourself or the person who hurt you?

Four of Swords

Book some time off work and lock your doors! The Four of Swords is directing you to take a break. You need some rest and alone time. Perhaps you need some space to heal after a loss or difficulty, maybe you've been ill, or things have simply been getting too much. This card is telling you it's time to regroup and give yourself time to recover the energy and focus you need to move on again.

Upright

An upright Four of Swords is a clear indication you need some time and space to rest up. If the demands of family and friends are all too much, or you're feeling disconnected from your partner in some way, take some alone time to get some relief and clarity. (This card might also be a reminder that if loved ones feel distant, it's probably nothing to do with you and more likely they're just going through something and need a little space too.) Or perhaps you've gone through a health scare, break-up, job or money loss, or other trauma and you need to take time off to recharge your batteries. Having some time with your own thoughts will help you regain energy and clear your mind. When you feel better, plan your next move but try to take things one step at a time.

Reversed

A reversed Four of Swords is telling you you're in danger of total burnout if you don't take a step back. You're running on empty, fuelled only by anxiety and stress, and you need to self-quarantine, now. Book a hotel, turn off your phone, lock your doors – do whatever you have to in order to get some peace and quiet and find your calm. When you re-enter the world, make sure to schedule in some regular meditation or alone time too.

This card reversed can also mean you feel frustrated or restless in some aspect of your life, perhaps in a relationship or change you've wanted to make that has been delayed. Take a break and come back to these situations when you're stronger and feel better able to make the changes you want.

———※———

Five of Swords

Do you run from any kind of tension or disputes or do you relish a quarrel and a chance to air your opinions? The Five of Swords card appears when it's time to evaluate the way you deal with conflict. Arguments and disagreements are an important part of life and there is no way to avoid them. Having said that, it's also better not to add fuel to the fire of any disputes and make difficulties worse. The Five of Swords is a reminder not to shy away from speaking up when we need to, but also not to fight just for the sake of it.

Upright

The upright Five of Swords is a warning not to let your anger spiral out of control. Pause to think about what effect your angry reactions and behaviour might have on you. If someone has let you down or hurt you, is hurting them back really going to help? Won't it leave you feeling lousy? It's good to speak your mind and express your feelings, but if that spills over into revenge or spite that's not the best way to go either. Addressing an issue honestly and carefully might break tension or prevent resentment building up, and it's good to stand up for yourself, but think about how you go about doing it. If you can do it in a positive way, great. If not, ask yourself if it'd be better to let it go.

Reversed

A reversed Five of Swords asks you to take a long hard look in the mirror and ask yourself if this really is a fight you want to take on. Is it even a struggle that needs to be tackled at all? If you can honestly and whole-heartedly say this is a conflict you need to address, then go for it. If not, steer well clear of it. This card reversed also encourages you to get better at accepting defeat. Life isn't a competition you always have to win.

Six of Swords

Pack your bags. It's time to go! The Six of Swords is the card of movement. It is telling you it's time to move on, either from the physical place you're in now or from a situation that's not working out. It can be hard to leave things behind and make a change, but the Six of Swords also reminds us that your destination will be more peaceful and happier than where you are now.

Upright

Drawing an upright Six of Swords means you're due for a transition of some kind. You might be relocating, travelling for business or pleasure, or moving towards or away from some kind of conflict. An upright Six of Swords can also mean you're moving towards a personal goal or change in your patterns of behaviour. Leaving behind a home, job or people is tough, especially if you haven't had much choice in the matter, but this card tells you this move will be a good one in the end. To get to your destination, you may need to release some of the emotional baggage you've been carrying around. Try to throw overboard any memories, relationships, bad habits or ideas that are holding you back from growth and development.

Reversed

The Six of Swords reversed can be drawn when things aren't moving forwards as you hoped they would. Perhaps you are struggling to discard a relationship, belief or pattern of behaviour that isn't good for you. Or maybe you know you are resistant to making the lifestyle change that you should because you don't want to face the difficulties involved or you resent being forced into it. Try to resolve the issues that are holding you back and focus on the benefits of the change instead.

This card reversed can also be a sign of unfinished business, whether that is unlearnt lessons from the past or lingering feelings for an ex. The Six of Swords reversed card reminds you a better future lies ahead, so do whatever you can to keep moving towards it.

Seven of Swords

Truth or lies? The Seven of Swords card is a cosmic warning that someone is being sneaky and deceitful. It's a sign that things may not be what they seem and someone acting for their own self-interest is hiding something important. Who is playing tricks and why are they using subterfuge to get what they want? Whatever the cause, this card is telling you that you need to put yourself first if you are going to be able to see the whole picture for what it really is and move forwards.

Upright

In love and relationships, the upright Seven of Swords may represent deception or a secret. That could mean a lover is cheating on you, or you are cheating on them. It could also suggest that a relationship would benefit from more honesty and open communication and fewer secrets. If you're single, it might mean that your crush isn't interested or that someone or something is standing in your way.

Drawing an upright Seven of Swords is a sign that there's a rocky road ahead. You should be prepared for some challenges at work or in your daily life. Watch your spending and watch out for difficulties with others at work. Rely on yourself to solve problems that come up.

Reversed

If you're looking for love, a reversed Seven of Swords card asks you to think about what's holding you back from finding a lasting relationship, or work out who or what is standing in your way. It could also be a caution not to let another person walk over or hurt you in a relationship or a sign that a relationship is nearly over.

The Seven of Swords reversed also warns you against using deception to get what you want, or to look out for someone who might be deceiving you. Don't be afraid to stand up for yourself, but don't play a deceitful game. Perhaps you have doubts about the way to proceed with a project, money decision or another move. This card reversed reminds you to proceed with caution and spend some more time thinking before going ahead.

Eight of Swords

You may not want to hear this, but you need to. The Eight of Swords is here to dish out a few painful home truths. It's a warning that you feel suffocated by a situation because of your own self-limiting beliefs or victim mentality. Is your negative self-talk or pessimistic outlook holding you back? This may be a hard pill to swallow but if we can see where the problems are, then we can also do something to fix them. You get to call the shots and define your own future, if only you stop causing problems for yourself.

Upright

Drawing an upright Eight of Swords card suggests you feel trapped and in a situation you can't get out of. You might be in a hole, but are you sure you didn't dig that hole for yourself? If you want to climb out, you first need to acknowledge your part in getting there. Whether you're being passed over for a job at work, or losing sight of yourself in a destructive love affair or friendship, this is your signal to take back your power. You need to change your perspective on it. You don't have to be a victim here. Stand up for yourself, leave the job or the relationship and work the problems through.

Reversed

Congrats! The Eight of Swords reversed tells you that you have been through some tough times but you have come out the other side. You have come to terms with the difficulties you faced and the bad habits or negativity that plagued you before. You are in a position to accept yourself for who you are and ready to start walking the path to the future. Don't overthink it. Accept the perspective shift you've achieved and go forth and conquer!

Nine of Swords

Another night spent tossing and turning, unable to switch your brain off from the worries and fears spinning around in it? The Nine of Swords card represents anxiety, depression or fear. It suggests you are at risk of being crushed under the weight of these miserable thoughts or desolate feelings. The more you worry, the worse the anxiety gets. It builds and builds, until it overwhelms you. The Nine of Swords warns you to find a way to break this destructive cycle.

Upright

An upright Nine of Swords cautions you against letting your worries and fears take over so much they actually cause the worst to happen. For example, you spend so much time worrying you can't do your job that you make mistakes. The danger of too much negative thinking is that those thoughts can become a reality.

This card reminds you that it is time to examine your situation from a new perspective. Instead of looking for evidence of what is going wrong, turn your attention to what is going right. Take a deep breath and realise that life is not as dreadful as it seems and that the more you worry, the more harm you are doing to yourself, especially if your worries are causing nightmares and stopping you from sleeping.

Reversed

A reversed Nine of Swords card suggests that your deep-seated fears are getting the best of you and you haven't been able to deal with your own inner turmoil by yourself. It's time to stop keeping your feelings a secret and confide in someone you trust. They will give you the help and support you need so you can deal with your self-limiting beliefs and self-doubt and feel better.

Alternatively, the reversed Nine of Swords can mean you have released the worries already and you've been able to see the situation through new eyes and with a fresh and more positive perspective.

Ten of Swords

It's time to be ruthless. The Ten of Swords means the hour has come when you must cut someone or something destructive from your life or move on from a situation that is causing you pain and trouble. This card is all about defending yourself, no matter what, and believing that even when your world feels like it is crumbling, you can find peace and happiness again.

Upright

An upright Ten of Swords is a sign that something in your life has come to a painful and possibly sudden end. Perhaps a partner has left you, you've been made redundant at work or an unfinished project has been pulled. Endings like this leave deep wounds. The grief and loss can feel even worse if the ending involved betrayal or deceit. Maybe your partner betrayed you by cheating on you or a so-called friend told lies about you. You're hurt by their behaviour and the fact that it means the end of the relationship.

Don't give up hope. You may have hit rock bottom but that means the only way is up. Change is in motion so all you can do is learn from it what you can and move on. Maybe some small part of you already knows it's for the best.

Reversed

Drawing a reversed Ten of Swords shows that you are resisting an inevitable change or ending brought on by a crisis. If you're ever going to get over this, you need to let it happen so you can start healing.

A reversed Ten of Swords card can also suggest that one reason you are finding it hard to accept something is over is that you are carrying scars from previous hurtful encounters or situations. You need to face the effects of past pains and see how your reactions to them are holding you back from choosing a new direction for yourself. After a storm or fire, it's time for regeneration, growth and development and you need to move forwards with a sense of renewal and hope.

———※———

Page of Swords

Yawn! We all get times when we're stuck in a rut and life feels a bit drab and boring. When the Page of Swords appears, that's a sign that dull and dreary is about to be replaced by wild and wacky! This card brings an energy that is bubbling over with curiosity and enthusiasm for what's next. It suggests you're due a fresh perspective and you should take the chance to try a different way of thinking. Life can be a wild ride if you go with it!

Upright

The upright Page of Swords is here to tell you to stop drifting through life and start discovering what it can offer you. It's time to try something different and new, so get out there and work out what that something is. Ask around, do some research, follow your nose wherever it leads. Look at your life and options from a new angle. Don't shut any options out just yet. Intrigued by a new hobby, career path, love interest? Chat, laugh, let loose a little. Open up and let yourself and others see how you feel and what inspires and excites you.

Reversed

The Page of Swords reversed suggests you are someone who doesn't have problems coming up with new ideas or inspiration, but you do struggle to stick with those plans long enough to make them actually happen. You bounce around excitedly when a new scheme pops into your brain, but that enthusiasm can suddenly switch to the next big idea, and the next. You need to stick with things a bit longer and with more determination. Try not to be so scatterbrained and focus on one thing at a time so that each idea has time to develop. Others will also appreciate the new way you stick to your promises and plans.

Knight of Swords

And... Action! (Imagine a movie clapperboard snapping shut here...) The Knight of Swords card is telling you it's time to make things happen. Go, go, go! Set your engine to full speed ahead and chase your dreams and desires with steely determination. This card is all about being energetic and ambitious but a word to the wise: before you enjoy the rush of that forward momentum, come up with a plan of action. Prioritise what you need to do and concentrate on the tasks that will make a real difference, so you don't end up wasting valuable time and energy.

Upright

The upright Knight of Swords points to this being your time to shine. You're on the way up! You know what you want and you're going all out to get it. It feels like nothing can stand in your way. You're bursting with ambitious energy but you're still keeping your head. You're working out the logical steps you need to take to reach your goal. You're laser-focused and ready to tackle any problems or challenges that you meet along the way. You are self-assured and assertive. You're going to make this happen!

Reversed

The Knight of Swords reversed suggests someone tends to act first and think later. It's great to be truly focused on a goal but if you go full speed ahead without making a plan or seeing what's going on around you, you're going to fail. Being single-minded and so intent on your own thing can also make you confuse being straightforward and direct with being rude and insensitive, and your interactions with other people might seem abrupt and disrespectful. You really need to slow down and give yourself time to follow your ideas through. Save some of that lively and excited energy to spend on tackling problems and dealing with other people politely and respectfully. Tame that impulsive nature, just a little!

Queen of Swords

The Queen of Swords is a card that implores us to look at things and say things as they really are. The only way you're going to make things better or achieve your goals is to be clear and honest, whether that's in relationships, business or day-to-day life. This card exhorts us to use our heads. Think before you act and scrutinise a situation carefully before taking action. Use your smarts, but also don't forget to have a laugh along the way. This queen is wise and wilful, but not boring.

Upright

In terms of your relationships, drawing a Queen of Swords upright is telling you to cut through the nonsense that's cluttering communication with friends, family or loved ones and speak with honesty and openness. Tell people truthfully what you need. Try not to judge yourself or others too harshly. We all have failings and make mistakes sometimes. Sort stuff out using your sharp wit and not your sharp tongue.

In a reading about careers or money, this card indicates you know what the right move is for you. Trust that you know what you're doing, based on past experiences and your instincts. You're smart and if you feel this is the right time for a career change, go for it.

Reversed

A reversed Queen of Swords card is a signal that you need to have a think about what it is you really want and need. Are you being honest with yourself? Once you're clear about what it is you're after, find your voice and say it. In relationships, that might mean letting your partner know you want to be exclusive. It may mean that something isn't right at work and you need to figure out what and set some boundaries or talk to someone about it.

The Queen of Swords reversed can also suggest that you're cutting yourself off from people, perhaps because of the challenges you haven't been able to address yet. Self-isolation isn't going to help. Give yourself some tough love and get back on with your life.

King of Swords

At a crossroads in life and not sure which direction to take? Or feeling confused about what's really going on in a relationship and don't know what to do? The King of Swords card is all about bringing some welcome straight talking and thinking into any situation. This card encourages us to examine situations with our head not our heart and to work out what's the best and fairest solution for everyone involved. When this card comes along, you can be sure that if you leave your emotions aside, you have the honesty and integrity to do what's right.

Upright

The upright King of Swords is telling you that you're letting your imagination run away with you and you're losing sight of what's really going on in your life. You're confused and don't know which way to turn, and the more you worry about it the worse that confusion gets, and the farther away you are from an answer. You need to look at the situation as if you were an impartial outsider. Leave your feelings out of it and be logical about your choices. Ask people directly for the information you need. Be a straight shooter. You'll feel empowered and able to make a move once you have the facts.

Reversed

A reversed King of Swords can be a warning to rein it in a little. Yes, you may know a thing or two but if you only ever listen to the sound of your own voice, you're going to annoy people and you'll never learn anything new. It's good to be a straight talker but don't risk coming off as mean and cruel and make sure you don't spill over into becoming judgmental of others (or yourself for that matter). This is a time for less talking and more listening. You'd do a lot better if you could only button your lip and listen to other people for a change.

Ace of Pentacles

Life doesn't always feel like it's full of possibilities, but the Ace of Pentacles is a card that offers just that. It alerts us to new opportunities and potential in our life and work. This card is a sign of good things to come. It's a signal that now is your chance to make money, advance your career, or even reach a new level of stability and security in your life. It is a cosmic heads-up that your dreams could come true if you take the chances being offered to you.

Upright

An upright Ace of Pentacles card tells you you're entering a time of plenty. The time is ripe for you to make changes to upgrade your work and wealth. So, if a new job or promotion comes your way, take it. Say yes to options that could boost your finances. But, don't expect overnight success. This card also serves as a reminder that things that are worthwhile take time and effort. Be patient and your dreams will come true.

While you're working towards your goals, or waiting to reach them, make time to work out and eat well too. Your health matters and you want to be at your best to enjoy your success when it comes.

Reversed

Are you suffering from imposter syndrome, even though deep down you have got what it takes to succeed? The reversed Ace of Pentacles often comes along to ask you why you're sabotaging yourself. If a new opportunity or job offer has arisen, what is preventing you from grabbing it with both hands? Are your doubts justified, or should you quit stalling and take the chances that the universe is offering to you? Of course it's wise to consider your options, but don't let misplaced fears hold you back too long.

A reversed Ace of Pentacles can also be a warning that you need to economise and make some spending cuts, just in case something changes. Things will settle down but maybe this isn't the right time to max out your credit cards.

Two of Pentacles

The Two of Pentacles is a card about the juggling act of life. It's about the way we often have to handle several things at once to make life work. It can be tough to keep all the balls in the air and balance the different parts of our world: work, family, relationships and a social life. The Two of Pentacles is here to remind us that with a little effort and focus we are perfectly capable of achieving the balance we desire.

Upright

An upright Two of Pentacles card is the universe's way of congratulating you on a job well done. You are managing to juggle multiple priorities and tackle the challenges that life throws at you along the way. However, like any juggler, it is easy to lose focus and drop one of those balls at any time. Don't get so caught up with coping that you don't also give yourself time to check in and make sure you're managing your time and priorities well. A pause can also give you a chance to see the whole picture and allow yourself more free time to see family or less free time so you can hit a deadline, for example. Be adaptable too, so you can balance different demands at different times.

Reversed

When the Two of Pentacles is reversed it brings a warning that you're losing control of things. Maybe you've taken on too much or you've become a little disorganised. This is causing you anxiety. It's time to reset your priorities. Sit down and make some lists and schedules to help you plan out your time. Work out what you can cancel to ease the stress.

This card can also suggest that your work-life balance is off. Perhaps you're spending too much time at work and not giving enough attention to your relationships. Take a step back and remind yourself what life you want. Focus on the thing that is most important to you, but don't forget to make time for the other stuff too.

Three of Pentacles

There is no 'I' in 'team'! The Three of Pentacles is a reminder that in work, sports, family or relationships, each person has their part to play. Teamwork happens when people work together towards a common goal. Though there are some situations where it's better to act alone, learning how to work together without conflict can help almost anyone achieve greater success. So, follow the lead of the Three of Pentacles and find harmony and happiness through cooperation.

Upright

An upright Three of Pentacles reminds us of the importance of diversity within a team. Everyone has something to offer and it's the sharing of a variety of ideas and opinions that yields the best results. For a team, family or relationship to work, people need to listen to each other, respect each other's opinions, and be ready and willing to learn from each other too.

This card also suggests that you have a goal in mind and you're ready to carry it out using the resources and people you have. Just make sure you have a good plan and everyone understands what that plan is. Then you're good to go!

Reversed

A reversed Three of Pentacles indicates that a team or relationship is falling apart and that you don't all have the same goals. Maybe people aren't listening to each other properly or being honest about their ideas or feelings? You need to take a pause. Ensure people are being respectful and agree what needs to be done. Make a detailed plan which everyone agrees to and set about achieving your shared goal.

This card can also hint that you're in the wrong team and maybe you need to switch to a role where your talents are better utilised and appreciated. Or perhaps it means you prefer to work alone. Flying solo might suit you, but don't shy away from asking for help when you need it.

Four of Pentacles

It's time to shake things up! The Four of Pentacles is a call to break with the past and try to tackle life in a fresh new way. We can all get set in our ways and repeat patterns of behaviour, even if they aren't working for us anymore. In particular, this card is often a signal to review attitudes towards money and material possessions and a warning to make sure these aren't taking priority over the friends, family and relationships that bring real, long-lasting happiness.

Upright

An upright Four of Pentacles implies you need to re-evaluate your money situation. It's not that you don't have enough money, rather that you may need to check you have the balance between life and money right. Are you working and saving hard but neglecting your relationships and relaxation, for example? It's important to save and live within your means, but you need to spend some money to enjoy life too. Avoid putting too much value on money and material possessions and not enough on people and happiness.

This card may also suggest you need to play it safe at work and in your personal relationships too. It's fine to stick at something that works, rather than risk ruining what you have, but don't be too closed off or inflexible.

Reversed

A reversed Four of Pentacles warns you that you care too much about money and things and you're now learning that you need good relationships to be happy. Perhaps you've even been overspending in an attempt to buy the happiness you seek. Or has greed taken hold of you and you're overdoing it at work to earn more and more? Instead of chasing money and filling your home with new stuff, look for love instead.

This card can also be a sign that you need to nest right now, finding some comfort in cleaning your space or reorganising your drawers. This kind of activity can be grounding when other things in life seem uncertain.

Five of Pentacles

You're a survivor. You may have been or may be going through a rough patch and you may be feeling lost and alone, but take heart. The Five of Pentacles is here to provide comfort and reassurance. Yes, it's a card that represents struggle, loss and financial hardship but it's also a reminder that things will improve and there are people out there who can give you help, if only you ask for it. It's time to get to the bottom of the problem, find your strength, and move forwards.

Upright

The upright Five of Pentacles asks you to take a cold, hard look at what your money worries are and what is causing them. You might constantly be feeling strapped for cash, but maybe the situation isn't that bad. If your bills are getting paid, then perhaps your worries are more to do with you not getting what you want rather than not getting what you need. In that case, you could relieve the stress by adjusting your frame of mind. If you are really in trouble financially, then make a plan to deal with it. Make or get help setting a budget and make some cutbacks and changes. It might not be easy at first, but it's better than all that stress and worry. If you're feeling alone, it's time to reach out. Someone you know will be glad to help.

Reversed

When the Five of Pentacles is reversed, it suggests your struggles are nearly over but it's not quite time to relax. If you're finding it hard to pay the bills, this card might be a sign you're going to get a bonus, a pay rise or a new job that will help you make ends meet. Or it could mean that your budget cuts are making a difference and you're getting back on your feet. If you've been ill, it's a sign you should get well soon. Things are getting better but you still have to keep on making an effort to keep them moving in the right direction.

Six of Pentacles

The Six of Pentacles represents success, wealth and generosity. Perhaps you've come in to some money recently or got a promotion or a new job that has brought you a happy new financial security. This card is a reminder to share some of that good fortune by being generous to others. It's a card about both giving and receiving. Things can change in the blink of an eye and it could be you who needs help in the future, whether that support is financial or emotional. Life is all about balance.

Upright

When the Six of Pentacles is drawn upright it suggests you're in a good place financially. Your account is in the black and you are even in a position to share your prosperity and help people in need. This might take the form of donations to a good cause or charity or helping a friend out. Your generosity might also be expressed by giving someone you know the extra love, time, expertise or physical help that they need.

It can also mean that it's you who is receiving financial aid or another kind of help from other people. Be grateful and appreciative of whatever help is being offered and use it as a chance to rebuild and become self-sufficient again.

Reversed

A reversed Six of Pentacles might be telling you to look out for yourself. Maybe you've been spending or giving other people more than you've got. Don't risk getting into debt. You need to make sure you're okay and give to yourself too.

This card can also suggest the cycle of giving and receiving is a little out of balance. Perhaps you've been helping someone out and they're not paying their debts or aren't showing any gratitude. Maybe it's time to cut off the assistance or find a way to ensure they do pay you back or understand the importance of appreciation.

Seven of Pentacles

Keep your eyes on the prize! The Seven of Pentacles card suggests that you have been working hard towards something and that effort is paying off. Your hard work and staying power has resulted in success and you deserve it. This card also reminds us that although it's good to persevere and be determined, it's important not to wear ourselves out in the pursuit of a goal.

Upright

An upright Seven of Pentacles is your excuse to start celebrating the success you have attained through hard work and patience. Or it could be that your hard work is just about to pay off. It is also a call to check your efforts are still being put to good use. It's time for a long-term view. If you've been working very hard, that may not be sustainable. What is it you want to achieve next and what is the best way to use your time and effort to get it?

On the other hand, this card can suggest you've invested a lot of time and effort, but you're not seeing the results you hoped for. Accept that it's going to take longer. Persevere and try to be grateful for what progress you've made so far.

Reversed

A reversed Seven of Pentacles suggests you lack focus and though you're trying hard, some of your efforts may be misplaced. You need a long-term goal or vision and a plan to achieve it that ensures some of your energy and efforts are not just being wasted. This card can also suggest you're having limited success. Perhaps stress and pressure outweigh rewards. Or you're simply not getting out of a situation what you hoped for. You don't have to keep plugging away if it's going nowhere. You can stop and take a new direction or drop the project altogether.

In terms of relationships, a reversed card says you may be feeling that you're putting in more work than the other person and it's not paying off anyway. You may need to ask yourself if this relationship is worth it...

Eight of Pentacles

You know when things are going wrong or you're feeling out of your depth, and a friend leans over and gives you a reassuring pat on the back? Like the Eight of Pentacles, that gesture is one of support and it's telling you that you've got this. It takes time and effort to achieve our goals and sometimes it feels like we'll never get to the finishing line, but this card is a reminder to keep going. You are nearly there!

Upright

Drawing an upright Eight of Pentacles suggests you are working hard to improve yourself or your skill set. This could mean taking on an apprenticeship or college course, changing jobs, or retraining in a new industry. It could also mean you're refining a more personal hobby, such as cooking, dancing or music, or that you're making some changes in your life to make you happier or more content. You know that these improvements or changes won't happen overnight, but you're prepared to keep going and to put in the time and effort necessary to make them happen. This card is here to reassure you that your efforts will pay off and you will find success and become the best person you can be.

Reversed

The reversed Eight of Pentacles often appears when you're focusing most of your efforts on self-development and improvement. You're taking an honest look at what you need to do to be the best you can be and you're putting in the effort to make those changes.

On the flip side, this card can also mean that this determination has crossed over into perfectionism. No one is perfect. Working too hard to achieve that is only ever going to end in frustration and failure and can make you lose sight of what's really important.

Alternatively, it can indicate that your progress is being held back in some way, perhaps because you don't have all the expertise you need or because some of your activities are misdirected. Check whether you're spending too much time on the wrong things and get back on track.

Nine of Pentacles

Give yourself a pat on the back. The Nine of Pentacles card indicates that you have reached a stage in your life where you are confident, independent and self-sufficient. You've worked hard and earned your success and you're now ready to kick back and relax and enjoy the money, leisure and material comfort you've gained.

Upright

The Nine of Pentacles upright means that you're in a good place and you shouldn't be afraid to spend some money on yourself or give yourself some time to do what you like. Splash some cash on a weekend away or some luxuries you've been lusting after. You have come a long way and while your journey isn't over, you should take a moment to celebrate where you are now. This card also suggests you've found a sense of independence and self-sufficiency too. You can take care of your money and you can take care of yourself. You don't need other people to support you. You've got this.

This feeling of harmony also spreads into other parts of your life. Perhaps you're feeling at one with nature or other parts of your life and relationships are feeling well-balanced also.

Reversed

A reversed Nine of Pentacles suggests you may be questioning your self-worth. Maybe you don't value yourself highly enough or have doubts about your abilities. Do you wonder if you can really do this job or if you'll ever meet 'the one'? This card reminds you that you do deserve success and fortune in every part of your life.

So, work on improving your self-belief. Do whatever it is you need to in order to boost your confidence and improve your chances of succeeding at work and in life. This could mean opening up or it could mean you talk to someone about the personal issues you need to address.

Ten of Pentacles

Can you hear that applause? You've reached a milestone on your journey and the Ten of Pentacles is here to remind you to enjoy a sense of accomplishment. You have taken some big steps towards the life you want, whether that is in your career, your financial stability, home life or relationships. Your hard work is bringing you money and you can also enjoy sharing this abundance with other people. Things are really starting to come together for you!

Upright

When you draw the upright Ten of Pentacles card, it means you're comfortable. You have stability in your life. No more scrimping and saving. You have financial security and can buy what you need. This card suggests this success won't be short-lived. If you keep going the way you are going, you will achieve long-term success. This sense of security means you feel able to support your family or loved ones and help friends out too.

The Ten of Pentacles upright also points to the fact that family stability is important to you and you have that as well. Family time brings you pleasure and you contribute to their lives and you to theirs in many different ways. You have a pride in your family history and tradition and relish that sense of belonging.

Reversed

The reversed Ten of Pentacles unveils the dark side of money. Being wealthy can make you want more and more, bigger and better. As your tastes get more expensive, you may spend too much of your hard-earned cash and risk losing it because you can't bear to give anything up. Don't lose sight of the fact that money isn't everything. Do you really want to work all the time just so you can feel rich?

This applies to your personal life too. Are you fighting too hard for something you don't really want? Maybe you think you want a serious relationship when really all you want is a good time for now. Are you doing a job you like, or the one you think you should do because it is more secure?

Page of Pentacles

Always look on the bright side of life. Drink from a cup that is half full, not half empty, as they say. The Page of Pentacles is an optimistic card. It suggests you're enjoying success in work, money or another part or parts of your life and you're on the way to achieving what you set out to do. To keep on track, you are going to have to keep hold of that momentum. Keep acting with enthusiasm and energy to see you through to the end. Keep that fire burning and stay focused. If you do, you will achieve success.

Upright

An upright Page of Pentacles indicates you're on track for a great career or financial success. Believe that anything is possible and use that energy and optimism to fire you up as you progress. This card is a sign you're able to make good, sound business or career decisions, so trust your instincts and follow your destiny.

In terms of relationships, this card upright suggests that you're in a good place. If you're in a long-term relationship, make sure you have some fun and bring some surprises into the mix to keep things fresh. And if you're single, take this card as a sign that it's time to follow your heart and make a match.

Reversed

A reversed Page of Pentacles card suggests things may not be going so well and the blame lies with you! Be honest. Do you have a tendency to be a bit lazy, impatient or immature? Do you get frustrated when things don't go your way instantly? You can fix this. Don't delay. If you can't make a change with willpower alone, ask for help.

Is your attitude affecting a relationship? If your boredom or indifference is more to do with you than them, try to work on the relationship you have before moving on. If your attitude is affecting your work, you need to make a plan and stick to it. Maybe you'll feel more motivated if you find a job that suits you better?

Knight of Pentacles

It may not sound as thrilling as overnight success, but there's a lot to be said for working hard and being determined to reach your goals. The Knight of Pentacles represents the serious work and effort it takes to achieve real dreams and ambitions. To get the job done, you might have to keep your head down and work hard and sometimes that work might be a bit dull or repetitive, but it will bring success.

Upright

When an upright Knight of Pentacles card is drawn, it is a sign that you have a plan of action and you're sticking to it. You're working hard and methodically and though progress may be slow you are not being deterred. You're sticking to your routine and gradually getting past the obstacles along the way. You will get the job done.

This card can also mean you have other demands on your life that can be a bit boring and tiring sometimes, such as household tasks or other obligations. But you manage to carry on without too many complaints and you're sticking to your path. Okay, life is a bit of a chore right now, but it'll be worth it in the end.

Reversed

A reversed Knight of Pentacles card is a sign you could use a bit more self-discipline in your life if you're going to achieve your goals. Make a plan and a schedule and stick to it, even if it gets boring sometimes. That could mean setting out an exercise routine to reach fitness goals or planning to spend a day a month on life admin to get your paperwork in order.

This card can also mean the opposite! Maybe you do have the self-discipline necessary to succeed but the routine you're following is sucking the joy out of your life. Maybe it's time to let your hair down and have some fun. All work and no play is no good for any of us, so get out there and see your friends and try some new experiences too.

Queen of Pentacles

Can anyone really have it all? A welcoming, happy home, a satisfying career and good relationships? Well, the Queen of Pentacles is here to help you find a way to have all of this and more. The Queen of Pentacles is a card about generosity, contentment and caring for yourself and others. This card is like a big warm hug, just when you need it.

Upright

A Queen of Pentacles upright card is a message from the cosmos telling you that taking care of yourself should be your number one priority. If you take care of yourself, you're better able to take care of all the other people and things in your life. Who can be generous and welcoming if they're frazzled and wrung out? It's also a reminder to stick to the ingredients for the true recipe for happiness. You don't need all the money and possessions, you need enough. Work hard enough to earn what you need and share and enjoy that. Then you won't be over-stretching yourself and you'll be able to make time for all the other people and things you want to do in life.

Reversed

A reversed Queen of Pentacles is a warning to stop looking to the future all the time and enjoy the moment. Focus on what's happening here and now and be present so you can enjoy the bounty you already have instead of worrying about what might or might not happen in the future. Instead, check what your priorities are right now and switch your effort and energy to achieving those targets and intentions. This card can suggest you're not living in the moment and enjoying what you have now, because you're too busy coveting what others have. Remind yourself of the things that really matter and go for those instead, and that will really bring you contentment in your life.